Essays and Poems on Spirituality and Transformation

Healing with Psychedelics

ESSAYS AND POEMS ON SPIRITUALITY AND
TRANSFORMATION

CHRIS BECKER

Healing with Psychedelics

Copyright © 2020 by Chris Becker

DISCLAIMER: The following information is intended for general information purposes only. The author and publisher do not advocate illegal activities but do believe in the right of individuals to have free access to information and ideas. Individuals should always see their health care provider before administering any suggestions made in the book. Any application of the material set forth in the following pages is at the reader's discretion and is his or her sole responsibility.

Publisher: True Way Press

道真

For further information visit: https://www.chrisbecker.org/

Book and Cover design by Bookcoverworld

Cover photograph by Kevin Menajang from Pexels

Library of Congress Control Number: 2020908434

ISBN: 978-0-578-67468-1

First Edition: July 2020

To the travelers who struggle with pain and confusion they don't deserve, yet instinctively walk toward health and freedom, guided by the healing power of love.

The cure to the pain is in the pain.

—*Rumi*

CONTENTS

This is a book filled with touching and blunt authenticity which makes me trust Chris's words. This is a book filled with solid and serious research which resounds with clarity and facts. Finally, this is a book filled with poetry which reaches my heart, my own struggle as a human being, and my own aspirations as a seeker for health; this makes Chris's voice trustworthy.

—Françoise Bourzat, Woodside, California, author of Consciousness Medicine

This is a book of intimacy—the shedding of stored trauma and the unveiling of the transformative power of love. Chris weaves stories, essays, and poetry into a tapestry of compassion and courage, as he shares his own journey with the healing potential of psychedelics. The teachings are powerful and subtle, direct and lyrical. Chris opens his heart and surrenders to the mystery.

—Janetti Marotta, Ph.D., author of 50 Mindful Steps to Self-Esteem *and* A Fertile Path

Chris Becker has given us a gift with his story of his personal journey of healing childhood pain and facing his alcohol addiction. Offering the reader an inside look at his experience of using mind-expanding medicine to face his deep-seated feelings of abandonment and loss that led to his addictions years later, highlights how this new treatment approach works. We have needed a new approach to addiction treatment. This is a welcome addition to the recovery literature.

—J. Patrick Gannon, Ph.D., Clinical and Performance Psychologist, San Francisco, California and author of Soul Survivors: A New Beginning for Adults Abused as Children

ACKNOWLEDGMENTS

With gratitude and love for my family and friends. Special thanks to my wife Nancy Andersen for encouraging me to seek healing help. My deep appreciation goes to Alex Theberge LMFT, who served as my skilled and kindhearted "above-ground" therapist. I'm grateful to Dr. Brenda Golianu for writing the Foreword and for her many helpful comments. Thanks go to my editor, Emily Moberg Robinson, Ph.D., for her insightful and caring craft. Bows to the many teachers I've been blessed to encounter.

Special thanks to my guide-therapist, who helped me release a painful and lonely past, allowing me to grow with medicine and love.

FOREWORD

No matter our walk of life, cultural background, family size, or education, the processes of growing up, adaptation, and integration often create a sense of alienation from our deeper sense of self. The path of psychological or spiritual healing usually involves striving to regain that sense of belonging and authentic experience.

In *Healing with Psychedelics*, Chris Becker beautifully describes his own search for wellness and vitality, as well as warns us gently about some of the pitfalls that can befall us as we seek this deeper connection to life around us. Becker's journey has taken place over 30 years of spiritual practice, psychological work, and professional achievement. *Healing with Psychedelics* describes his deep and pervasive sense of pain rooted in childhood trauma, but also the joy and freedom coming from his long journey of healing. This is not a book written by someone who has had a passing insight or stumbles into a realization. Rather, Becker has taken the time to develop and anchor his realizations in the ground of his life.

Under professional guidance, Becker judiciously used psychedelics, medications that he sometimes terms entheogens, as part of his therapeutic experience. Entheogens enabled Becker to integrate the complex and sometimes painful elements of his personal history so he could experience wholeness in this everyday life.

This work serves as a powerful personal testament to the potential therapeutic benefit of this class of medications. Evidence is accumulating in the scientific literature for the use of psychedelic medications for treatment of pain, depression, anxiety, post-traumatic stress disorder, addiction, and other conditions. This volume is an important contribution to the discussion of the rational use of psychedelics to assist in personal growth, the treatment and cure of mental health ailments, and spiritual development and transformation.

In an even more holistic sense, Becker has combined several practices—Zen meditation, psychotherapy, and entheogenic work—to transcend a basic sense of isolation and pain into a recognition of the commonalities of human experience, allowing for a greater sense of wholeness, compassion, and connectedness to occur.

Dr. Becker brings a sense of uncompromising honesty and presence to his deep spiritual search for meaning, healing, and transcendence. For this effort and for his courage in relating his direct experience, we are all deeply grateful. This work is pioneering in the depth and clarity of the first-person description of the healing and transformation process that is part of our common human experience. We look forward to more contributions of this type in the years to come.

Brenda Golianu, M.D., Pain Specialist

INTRODUCTION

The statue and flowers
On the holy altar
Can't compare to my friends

Welcome to my collection of essays and poems. Here, I reflect on healing childhood psychological injuries and trauma with the help of talk therapy and psychedelic-assisted therapy. I describe in detail my personal journey of healing and spiritual growth, with the intent that the complex fabric of my life and transformation may help others with their own journeys. I write about exploring and opening up to spirituality; and I include some unconventional discussions of meditation.

Although the essays were written over a period of nine months, they reflect many years of exploration and struggle. My journey is complex, just as everyone's is. In fact, although no two person's paths are exactly the same, it may be this sometimes-drab and sometimes-vibrant tapestry of suffering and searching that we share which will bring the two of us together.

The searching, the meditation, the talk psychotherapy, the psychedelic-assisted therapy, and the wondering, crying, hoping, trying, and star-gazing—all these together formed a strong web that has sustained me.

I want to make it clear from the outset that this book has a happy outcome. The power of psychedelic medicine, sacred medicine, when used in the context of a wise, established tradition, and administered by a well-trained therapist-guide, has changed years into hours and hours into timelessness. Furthermore, a deep CONNECTION with the guide is a huge part of the healing and growth and shouldn't be overlooked.

And although I focus on healing childhood psychological injury or trauma, the healing work I describe also applies to trauma suffered by adults. In fact, this book offers hope to all individuals who wrestle with anxiety, depression, addiction, or physical ailments, but who don't know the origins of their suffering.

Most of us have experienced emotional pain in our childhood that radically changed our lives. However, too often this pain is repressed; we don't remember that anything damaging happened to us, let alone understand its manifestations on a conscious level. In *Healing with Psychedelics*, I often use the word "trauma" to describe how childhood psychological pain changes how we operate in the world. By "trauma," I am referring to a broad spectrum of adverse experiences and conditions, from horrific abuse, to living with an emotionally absent or needy parent, to being exposed to subtle but persistent and life-altering behavior "corrections." The trauma may not be from a parent; it could have come from an aunt or uncle, an older brother who hated or molested you, a terrible bully on the playground, or a teacher who ridiculed you. My definition is based on the premise that if a childhood experience changed who you are, it constitutes trauma.

Many of us believe we had a happy—or at least an "okay"— childhood, when, in fact, our childhood might better be described as a loss of or disconnection from our true self. As infants or young children, we were forced to create this false self in order to survive in and adapt to a world that didn't welcome us as we naturally were. This means that we now live and act unconsciously through a false persona, a "false self." Some would say we wear a mask or a suit of armor.

Chances are, if you've read the title and picked up this book, your true self, the self you were born to be, wants to escape the dungeon it's been locked in all these years. It doesn't matter if you are in your twenties or eighties or anywhere in between. It doesn't matter whether a clear or cloudy feeling is flowing through you. If this title is of interest, it's because there's a sense that something is missing. But it may take more than a simple key to open the door and release your inner child, this true self that needs to be loved as the beautiful person you originally were and always have been. It may take more than a crowbar, a jackhammer, or a stick of dynamite to get that door open. It may take psychedelics—powerful medicines used under the guidance of a skilled therapist.

If you are uncertain about what I'm saying, let's review the symptoms that reveal the inner emptiness that comes from being forced to live a false life. These may include the abuse of alcohol or drugs, other destructive behaviors like overeating, anorexia, or gambling, or addiction to shopping, money, power, success, fast cars, sports, or work. Knowing that DENIAL is common to these conditions, please take a moment and take honest stock of yourself. You may have unstable relationships. You may need lots of sex, or sex in a certain way. You may be depressed, or consumed with anxiety, or engage in compulsive behavior; perhaps you even have suicidal thoughts. These symptoms don't lie. If any of them sound familiar, you are suffering. You know this deep within. You may be trying to feel normal or to manage your suffering with addiction; you may "like" the addictive substance or behavior. However, there is no escaping the reality of the pain inside, even if you are trying to keep it at bay.

I've traveled through this pain. But before I talk about how I've come out on the other side, I need to tell you a bit about my background.

I bring the perspective of a scientist and long-time meditator. I possess credentials: a Ph.D. in chemistry from UC Berkeley, an MIT postdoc in chemistry and physics, about 130 peer-reviewed scientific journal articles, 20 U.S. patents. I've run a laboratory, managed groups, and co-founded two companies. I've been a meditator for about 30 years; mostly Zen style, but I know and respect Insight (Vipassana) meditation and other traditions. My credentials are insignificant compared to the divine light, but they are of some use—they let you know that I know some things, have some experience.

Science and meditation turn out to be a comfortable fit, in my opinion. Scientific training teaches careful, open-minded observation of nature. Meditation teaches careful, open-minded observation of our inner nature, our own consciousness. Science usually doesn't go there, but its emphasis on training and objectivity are helpful.

My life's journey has been one of twists and turns, hiding and exploring, cowardice and bravery, confusion and clarity. It's a journey we all are on in one way or another. We each have this life to understand, our own puzzle to unravel. Some of us know it; some of us don't. Most of us need help, and there's nothing shameful about that. Most of us have been disconnected from the inherent truth of who we are, and consequently, we need to rediscover it by visiting the source of our disconnection.

A lot of people are waking up now. There's something in the air. We are rousing from hibernation, rubbing sleep from our eyes, adjusting to the sunlight, feeling hungry for what's been missing. What are the next steps?

We can start by seeking help. This can be difficult, especially in America—the myth of the self-reliant individual who pulls himself up by his bootstraps has created a culture of stigma and shame about mental health issues. The prevailing assumption is that if you need psychotherapy, then there's something wrong with you. And the implication is that it's your fault, you're messed up, and that you should be ashamed of yourself. You're weak, pathetic, defective. This is a sick lie. The truth of the matter is that almost ALL of us need some mental health help. There's nothing shameful about it.

There are other barriers to seeking psychotherapy, of course. It costs money. But if you can afford it, or if you can pay on a sliding scale, it's money very well spent. This is your life and happiness we're talking about. Is there anything more important? There also is the issue of finding the right person. Not all therapists are highly skilled, and not every highly skilled therapist is right for you. So, you do need to take care; check references and ask about training and experience. It's important to be comfortable with your therapist, because in time, you really will have to be completely honest and vulnerable, holding nothing back.

In *Healing with Psychedelics: Essays and Poems on Spirituality and Transformation*, I reflect on my personal journey through meditation and psychedelic-aided psychotherapy. Major themes include spirituality, healing trauma, personal transformation, courage, and truth. Courage was needed to begin the path to transformation, to reflect honestly about myself and my behavior, to be vulnerable and seek help. I could not successfully tread the path to transformation without realizing the truth of who I originally was born to be, the false self I created in order to survive, the detailed nature of my injuries, and the power of love to heal.

My essays and poems cover a wide range of experiences and ideas, but all are encompassed by this circle of love.

In my essay "A Public Service Announcement," I review the scientific findings about adverse childhood events (ACEs) collated by the U.S. Center for Disease Control (CDC). About two-thirds of the general population have suffered from ACEs—and that's not even the full picture. There are more subtle forms of negative childhood experiences that cause us to behave in an artificial way and create a false self. In my case, my trauma wasn't so subtle, but my memory and feelings were mostly repressed. I needed to do substantial work, with the aid of medicines, to bring them up into my consciousness so healing could take place.

I have spent thousands of hours in sitting meditation. I describe the results of my meditation, give some advice to meditators, and discuss my perspective on Buddhism in various pieces throughout this collection, notably "Spiritual Reporter on the Divine Light," "Three Common Problems," "Love and Buddhism," "Tasty Food," and "The Role of Faith." I'm a huge proponent of meditation and mindfulness. However, I also have suffered from "spiritual bypassing," which is when people attempt spiritual practice without attending to their unresolved psychological wounds. Spiritual bypassing is very dangerous. That's why I highly recommend psychotherapy for anyone planning to get serious about meditation (or anyone else, for that matter). The consequences of spiritual bypassing are laid out in stark terms in "The Koan of Abuse by Spiritual Leaders."

A considerable part of this book explores psychedelic-assisted psychotherapy. "Psychedelics" is the commonly used word for substances like psilocybin, but I also use the term "entheogen," a psychoactive substance ingested for spiritual revelation and growth. I include MDMA in the psychedelic and entheogen categories, although MDMA is also sometimes defined as an empathogen, a psychoactive substance that produces feelings of emotional openness (heart-opening) and empathy. My therapy benefited immensely from ALL of my journeys with both MDMA and psilocybin mushroom medicines. "Spiritual Reporter on the Divine Light" describes my first journey with the heart-opening MDMA. It blew the doors off my emotions; it was if a glass cage I was living in suddenly shattered, and I was freed. The poems "Abandonment" and "Revelation" are testaments to the power of MDMA-assisted therapy. I hope others are so blessed.

I also report on three subsequent psilocybin journeys and their healing and cleansing effects in the "Celestial Washing Machine" series, describing my journeys with the mushroom earth medicine. The healing and spiritual power of this sacred medicine is enormous. It took me to where I needed to go, even though I had no idea beforehand that the journey was necessary or even possible.

I need to be very clear. My use of these psychoactive substances has been strictly for spiritual growth and psychotherapy—serious and careful work in conjunction with therapy and in the presence of an experienced therapist-guide. Not play, but work. This work is difficult, but it is always rewarding, healing.

Throughout most of my adulthood, I didn't appreciate how desperately I needed to (re)discover my true self, to heal my childhood trauma. I had no idea such a transformation was possible. But I have gone on an amazing journey. I hope you find my experience instructive and encouraging. May it even inspire you to begin your own journey into self-discovery and healing.

Santa Clara, California, USA
2020

EMPTINESS

Emptiness is a Buddhist term
That means we're all together.
Emptiness is a people term, too,
That means you have a hole in your heart.
This is a problem if you're a people.
So what do people do? Mostly
Try two things at once without even knowing –
Surround it so it can't be seen
And blindly try to fill it.
They hide it from others and even themselves.
I surrounded mine with wine bottles.
Some of them had pretty labels,
And the good wine tasted good.
"Ahhh," I would say as I took that first sip,
And some of the wine would run into the hole
but it would always leak out, never filled it.
People surround that hole with lots of things.
Almost anything you can imagine.
Not just drugs and alcohol, but
Food, shopping, sex, power, money,
The list is endless.
Included are yoga and meditation.
Even spirituality can be an escape
From the hole in your heart.

How did the hole get there?
You are to blame, it's your ancient karma.
Just kidding. Maybe you fell for that.
It would be easy to fall for that, and

Fall into the hole and curl up
And want to die. Want to escape
But not know how or where to,
Or just give up, build the wall even higher
Then jump off.

But I wouldn't write
If the hole couldn't be filled.
First step, beautiful person,
know there is no original sin.
That's a torture, sinful arrow, made from black.
You didn't make the hole.
You were whole and beautiful,
And even now beautiful still,
Can never be anything else.

To find the hole,
That comes next.
Peer over the wall,
Through the disguise,
Part the bushes.
It's not so easy but you can do it.
Be your own detective
With guides to help you
Follow the clues,
The clues are your feelings.
Follow the pain –
Start with the outer edges,
Travel downward,
Deeper and deeper,
Darker and darker.

Feel the contours,
Even finer, the fingerprints,
How it happened,
Who did that to you,
Made that pain,
Painful hole in you.
How you got disconnected
From your very self.

To fill the hole, first
You need a bottom.
That happens spontaneously
When you know you've
Reached the bottom,
The source of pain,
Where it all went wrong.

Then fill the hole
With love.
Guides can help
You get in position,
But it's between
You and God,
You and the Universe.
When you understand,
Open your heart
And surrender
To her love.
It rushes, gushes,
Tears of release
Coming streaming,

Flooding the broken streams
Until they merge into a
Vast river of new life.
Emptiness no more.

A PUBLIC SERVICE ANNOUNCEMENT

I have some bad news to share. The United States Centers for Disease Control (CDC) has determined that most of you reading this have a serious illness that will last for many years, if not the remainder of your life. It may quite likely result in your early death. Your physician has no cure for you; there is no drug to lessen your suffering.

You haven't heard about this terrible malady before? Perhaps you missed the headlines.

Is it a new coronavirus that has previously gone undetected? Has it been lying dormant in the nucleus of your cells, waiting to be activated by a new strain? No, it's not that simple.

I'm referring to childhood trauma, described by the CDC rather euphemistically as "Adverse Childhood Experiences" (ACEs). Haven't heard of these? Most people haven't, even though ACEs are the largest contributing factor to disease and sickness in this country. It turns out that an estimated two thirds of us have been unloved and injured when we were defenseless children. And personally, I think the two thirds may be an underestimate.

In 1998, the CDC and Kaiser Permanente jointly published the first study on ACEs, using the confidential survey data of 17,000 individuals, mostly white, middle-class, college-educated adults in Southern California. Since then, physicians and psychologists have published more than 2,000 peer-reviewed studies on the causes and effects of Adverse Childhood Experiences.

What exactly are ACEs? According to the CDC, ACE is the term for any abuse, neglect, and other trauma experienced by people under the age of 18. These can take many forms. Physical abuse includes, among other things, hitting, kicking, and shaking. Sexual abuse is pressuring or forcing a child to engage in sexual acts, or exposing them to a range of sexual activities. Emotional abuse is behavior that damages a child's emotional well-being and sense of self-worth; this may include actual abandonment, threats of abandonment or violence, shaming, name calling, withholding love and physical affection, and other forms of psychological maltreatment. Neglect is the failure to meet a child's physical and emotional needs for things like proper housing, medical care, food, and clothing. Other examples of ACEs include witnessing violence against a mother or other adult female; substance abuse by a parent or other household member; mental illness suffered by a family member; a suicide attempt by or death of a parent or other household member; the incarceration of a parent or other household member; and parents' separation or divorce.

Many children suffer very severe ACEs during their pre-memory and/or pre-verbal stages of life, before they turn four years old. Moreover, while an ACE can be a single traumatic event that happens on a particular day, ACEs also can last weeks, months, or years. In fact, a great majority of the children who have one ACE go on to experience multiple adverse events – 87%, by one research estimate.

The consequences of Adverse Childhood Experiences are long lasting, often persisting throughout an individual's entire life. ACEs are linked to early death, chronic health conditions, risky health behaviors, and a variety of psychological maladies. For example, ACEs lead to much higher rates of alcohol and drug abuse, smoking, and other forms of addictive behavior; cancer, diabetes, and heart disease; depression, anxiety, suicide, and other afflictions.

So far, I've been speaking about the consequences of ACEs for individuals. But children grow up and enter platonic, familial, and romantic relationships. What about these relationships? You can guess—it's not a good story.

Briefly, people who have suffered traumatic experiences during their childhood often end up with what is known as insecure attachment style, "a relationship style where the bond is contaminated by fear" (exploringyourmind.com). As adults, they find it difficult to trust and be intimate with others; this leads to unstable relationships, especially romantic relationships. Depression, anxiety, and substance abuse and other addictions also interfere with maintaining healthy relationships. These maladaptive behaviors are driven from deep within the unconscious mind, formed during childhood exposure to ACEs.

My good friends, calling this a public health crisis is not an exaggeration. And if two thirds or more of you reading this have suffered ACEs, as research has established, then what? If you aren't already aware of your past in this regard, a first step is to take an ACE questionnaire to help learn more about your own childhood experiences and how they may be affecting you today. A copy of the questionnaire can be found at the end of this essay and online. While the questionnaire is truly valuable, it does have limitations. Keep in mind that many childhood traumas occur pre-memory or are repressed—they are not easily accessed. Also consider that some traumatic experiences are more subtle than the ones indicated on the questionnaire. Even these more subtle experiences may have undermined your belief that you were valued or welcomed in the world as you truly are. These experiences may not necessarily have been incurred through someone's conscious or purposeful action, although in some cases that may be so.

It is fitting that the CDC, which is well known for its work on communicable diseases, is researching and tracking ACEs. It has been documented that childhood trauma is passed down from generation to generation. Some people believe this happens spiritually or epigenetically. I don't know about that, but it is clear that trauma is passed on—that is, re-created—by behavior. And given the prevalence of ACEs in the United States, calling this an epidemic is appropriate.

Why is this happening? Is there something about American culture that makes us so vulnerable to ACEs? What are the childrearing methods we use and philosophies we adhere to that cause so much damage? Is there something in American culture that predisposes us to abuse our children, and for them to pass this abuse on to their children?

Yes, there is. I would argue that American religious culture plays a significant role in our ongoing epidemic of ACEs. And although other religious and atheist traditions also saddle their children with lifelong guilt and dysfunction, in the United States (and elsewhere), we can look to widespread (mis)application of Christian beliefs as a major source of societally sanctioned childhood trauma.

Most of the behaviors that perpetuate this trauma actually are unspoken and unwritten. However, we can see its cultural institutionalization manifested in the following well-known sayings:

- ◆ Spare the rod and spoil the child (Proverbs 13:24).
- ◆ You are born with original sin.
- ◆ Children should be seen and not heard.
- ◆ Go to your room until you feel better.
- ◆ You need a time-out.
- ◆ What's wrong with you?
- ◆ You should know better.
- ◆ Stop crying.

- Boys don't cry.
- I'll give you something to cry about.
- You're being selfish.
- It's for your own good.
- Because I said so.
- You're making me sad.
- You don't mean that.
- You don't feel that way.
- Shame on you.
- You're fat.
- I'll leave if you keep doing that.
- I'll take you to the orphanage if you don't stop.
- Honor thy father and mother (Leviticus 19:3).

You'll notice that I began and ended the list with quotes from the Bible. I believe we have the hint of the answer here. American childrearing philosophy is heavily rooted in Puritan ideology and biblical concepts. In her book *The Body Never Lies: The Lingering Effects of Hurtful Parenting*, Alice Miller characterizes the commandment "Honor thy mother and father" as a kind of blackmail, a way to fetter children to a dishonest and blinding relationship with their parents. That commandment ought to be "Thou shall honor thy children." Well, none of the Ten Commandments address how to love or raise our babies and children.

Societies like the United States that have such strong Biblical roots just don't have the attitude that babies come first. We pay lip service to the idea that children are important. But we do not say, "Drop everything; the baby is crying." Or,

"There is nothing more important than my baby, my child." Or, "I will treat my child with complete honor and respect." Or, "I bow down to the beauty and innocence of my baby." Until our society prioritizes defending the defenseless, abuse will continue, trauma will continue, ACEs will continue.

As the list shows, there are many, many ways to hurt a child. It is easy to recognize patterns of physical abuse, such as beating, slapping, and spanking. But there are endless less obvious forms of abuse, too. Even "progressive" parents can injure their children without realizing it. For example, they might be aghast at the thought of spanking their child, but frequently use time-out—actions of isolation and rejection—as a way to "manage" their child's behavior. Shooting disapproving glares, or simply looking away when the child wants you to see them, can cause emotional damage. Not answering a baby's cry, and thereby denying its need for emotional connection, is perhaps the most heartbreaking act to meditate on. All of these dysfunctional and distant parenting strategies have their roots in authoritarian and repressive traditions.

Normal child development includes a prepubescent narcissistic phase. During this time, if something is wrong in their world, children believe it is their fault. If their parents are arguing, it's because of something the observing child did. If a mother isn't loving towards her baby, then the infant internalizes the blame, developing a belief that there is something wrong with them. Once we understand this developmental phase, it is easy to see how readily adults can hurt children, perpetrate ACEs, and force children to hide/alter their true selves.

But why is the trauma passed on generationally? Psychologists like Miller can provide better and more complete explanations than I can. However, it's clear that ignorance about healthy parenting methods is a major factor; hence, the importance of education. There is also a linked chain of behaviors—some of us call it karma—in which internalized rage or shame from one's own childhood manifests in child rearing.

If you conclude that you or a loved one has suffered childhood trauma, you can do something about it. Many turn to multiple romantic partners, alcohol or drugs, overeating, anorexia, or other forms of addiction to manage the pain below the surface; these only lead to more suffering and poor long-term physical and mental health. However, it is possible to heal. A good psychotherapist can be a tremendous help. Although they are not magic pills, powerful medicines like MDMA and psilocybin, when used in the context of psychotherapy, also can be tremendously healing. And while I believe it generally is not sufficient by itself, meditation can be extremely helpful.

Healing takes work. And at least two thirds of us need to do this work. We only have so much time on earth. If you aren't already on the path of healing, won't you please start today? And once you've embarked on this path, you also will be able to help the next generation of children.

The first commandment reads, "You shall not have any gods before me." In order to protect and nurture our young, perhaps we should rephrase this commandment, saying instead: "My baby is God." But don't say this merely as motivation to work hard to be a good parent or caregiver. Rather, say this in the understanding that it is the literal truth.

REFERENCES

For information and other resources, see the Adverse Childhood Experiences page on the CDC website including links to the original journal article, select subsequent studies, and other resources. https://tinyurl.com/CDCstudyACE

Felitti, Vincent J et al. (1998). Relationship of Childhood Abuse and Household Dysfunction to Many of the Leading Causes of Death in Adults. American Journal of Preventive Medicine, 14(4), 245 - 258.

Miller, Alice. *The Body Never Lies: The Lingering Effects of Hurtful Parenting*. W. W. Norton & Company; Reprint edition (2006).

Firestone, Lisa (2013, June 30). How Your Attachment Style Impacts Your Relationship [Web article]. Retrieved August 10, 2019, from https://psychologytoday.com

(2018, February 20). Insecure Attachment – the 3 Different Types [Web article]. Retrieved August 10, 2019, from https://exploringyourmind.com

The ACE questionnaire can also be found at https://tinyurl.com/questionnaire-of-ACEs

Adverse Childhood Experience (ACE) Questionnaire
Finding your ACE Score ra hbr 10 24 06

While you were growing up, during your first 18 years of life:

1. Did a parent or other adult in the household **often** ...
   Swear at you, insult you, put you down, or humiliate you?
   or
   Act in a way that made you afraid that you might be physically hurt?
   Yes No   If yes enter 1 _____

2. Did a parent or other adult in the household **often** ...
   Push, grab, slap, or throw something at you?
   or
   Ever hit you so hard that you had marks or were injured?
   Yes No   If yes enter 1 _____

3. Did an adult or person at least 5 years older than you **ever**...
   Touch or fondle you or have you touch their body in a sexual way?
   or
   Try to or actually have oral, anal, or vaginal sex with you?
   Yes No   If yes enter 1 _____

4. Did you **often** feel that ...
   No one in your family loved you or thought you were important or special?
   or
   Your family didn't look out for each other, feel close to each other, or support each other?
   Yes No   If yes enter 1 _____

5. Did you **often** feel that ...
   You didn't have enough to eat, had to wear dirty clothes, and had no one to protect you?
   or
   Your parents were too drunk or high to take care of you or take you to the doctor if you needed it?
   Yes No   If yes enter 1 _____

6. Were your parents **ever** separated or divorced?
   Yes No   If yes enter 1 _____

7. Was your mother or stepmother:
   Often pushed, grabbed, slapped, or had something thrown at her?
   or
   Sometimes or often kicked, bitten, hit with a fist, or hit with something hard?
   or
   Ever repeatedly hit over at least a few minutes or threatened with a gun or knife?
   Yes No   If yes enter 1 _____

8. Did you live with anyone who was a problem drinker or alcoholic or who used street drugs?
   Yes No   If yes enter 1 _____

9. Was a household member depressed or mentally ill or did a household member attempt suicide?
   Yes No   If yes enter 1 _____

10. Did a household member go to prison?
   Yes No   If yes enter 1 _____

Now add up your "Yes" answers: _____ **This is your ACE Score**

ABANDONMENT

When as a child we're abandoned
Or threatened with abandonment,
We live in an unsafe world,
A place that does not welcome
Or accept us as we are.
Being ourselves is not possible,
It's a matter of survival.
So we block our true self
With a low sense of value,
A life of doubt and uncertainty.
We engage in activities
To show our parents
That we're worthy to enjoy
The love and acceptance we missed.
We must be successful in something
Rather than the beautiful person we are.
But it's a hollow victory if we can
Pull that off, and maybe we can't.
When the world is an unsafe place
We can't trust, can't trust others,
Can't trust a partner.
Not possible
Because a dark curtain surrounds us,
So dark it's hidden from view.
It's to protect ourselves,
Can't let others in, not safe,

So fear of intimacy pervades
The unconscious and anger
Bubbles up when affection is denied,
And affection is inevitably denied
When intimate giving is blocked.
Not safe here, better leave, broken.

How to heal, can you heal,
Only love can heal.
Best with someone close
Holding you while you visit
That pain of abandonment,
The darkest moment of terror
And they tell you
I'm not going anywhere.
Only love can heal

THE KOAN OF ABUSE BY SPIRITUAL LEADERS

*Koan: a paradoxical riddle
used as a teaching tool in Zen Buddhism*

Over the last few decades, Buddhists have been forced to acknowledge instances of abuse and unwholesome behavior perpetrated by their spiritual leaders—individuals (all men, by the way) who were believed to have attained enlightenment, or at least were considered to have spiritual authority. How is that possible? That is the koan, the puzzle.

Let's begin with some well-known examples that have been discussed openly in publicly available writing. Of course, there must be more we don't know about. (Perhaps abuse is like an infestation of cockroaches—where you see one, there are many more. We've already found this out in the Catholic Church.)

There's the well-documented case of Taizan Maezumi, who was associated with the Zen Center of Los Angeles. Maezumi played a major role in bringing Zen to America—and he also abused alcohol and was guilty of sexual misconduct. Revered Zen leaders Richard Baker, Dainin Katagiri, Eido Shimano, and Joshu Sasaki are reported to have been sexual predators. Chögyam Trungpa, the famous Tibetan Buddhist teacher, engaged in extreme alcohol abuse and sexual misconduct. Author and speaker Alan Watts, instrumental in popularizing Zen in America, also abused alcohol. All of these men were addicted to alcohol and/or unwholesome sexual behavior. Given their history, it is reasonable to presume that they also were addicted to power—a common element of this psychological dysfunction. Further, once a leadership role has been attained, the accompanying power and/or adoration amplify the person's ego and all its attendant dysfunctions.

It is difficult to reconcile these Buddhist leaders' significant spiritual insight with their extreme unwholesome behavior. So let's take a step back and consider the average man or woman who is addicted to alcohol, drugs, sex (in various manifestations), shopping, eating, gambling, money, power, etc. Why are they addicted? Is it because they lack moral fiber? Is there a hungry ghost living inside them and they just need an exorcism? I subscribe to the teaching of addiction expert and author Dr. Gabor Maté. He says that if you want to understand these behaviors, don't ask why the addiction; rather, ask why the pain. His perspective is that addiction is an attempt to feel normal, to feel whole (to reconnect with oneself), and to manage pain.

Ok; so why the pain? Maté's and others' research shows that dominating pain, enough to drive addiction, comes from trauma—and frequently, it comes from early childhood trauma. If you assume that trauma is the root of the pain and that the pain is driving addiction, then the next question becomes, "Why couldn't these spiritual leaders heal their pain?" It is certainly possible, though not easy, for people to heal from trauma. And you would think that highly trained spiritual leaders, well versed in mindfulness and lovingkindness meditation, would be able to heal their trauma. Right? Well, yes.

So now we come to the koan within the koan. Why didn't these spiritual leaders heal their trauma when they were experts in methods to do so? Ready for the answer?

BECAUSE THEY COULDN'T SEE THEIR EARLY CHILDHOOD TRAUMA. They didn't realize they had experienced life-altering trauma. They likely didn't have clear, conscious memories. If they did know they had a "difficult" childhood, they didn't understand how the pain changed how they behaved in the world. The path to their trauma was residing in their unconscious; it was underground, repressed. A good psychotherapist would have helped them find it, but alas, apparently, these leaders didn't have good psychotherapists. Although they had practiced years of meditation, this meditation did NOT help them find their buried trauma. It is worth noting that trauma-wounded individuals often sense that something is wrong, and they are drawn to religion or other organizations or practices in an effort to relieve their subsurface pain. But since they had performed what John Welwood calls a "grand spiritual bypass" around their own developmental problems, their childhood trauma went unsolved. It persisted through addictive behavior and created great pain and suffering. (Spiritual bypass is the pursuit of spiritual practice without attending to unresolved psychological wounds.)

This koan is not an intellectual curiosity for me, and I take no delight in solving it. That's because before I could understand the unwholesome behavior of these spiritual leaders, I had to solve my own painful koan. My insight into their puzzling behavior resulted from understanding my own. Here is my story.

I am now in my mid-sixties. I sought out Zen Buddhism in my mid-twenties and have practiced zazen (sitting meditation) and mindfulness for many years. I've had spiritual insights, and zazen has had a strong, positive effect on me, but nevertheless... I have suffered my whole life from addictive behavior and (romantic) relationship problems.

My addiction largely was to alcohol, which both provided the warm feeling that was missing from my childhood and numbed the pain of being unloved and unwelcomed as an infant and small child. I used alcohol for self-medication. "Ahhh," I would say to myself when I took that first, almost ceremonial sip, sinking into the comfort that I was anticipating. I also went through periods of significant marijuana use, again as self-medication to escape from pain. I remember liking alcohol and pot more than most of my peers did. I didn't understand why, and I didn't spend time worrying about it. I was more interested in getting high or drinking. But alcohol, and quitting it, is what brought me into psychotherapy.

Just to clarify, I kept my alcohol use within a functional limit. Never drank on the job. Never had a DUI. No physical withdrawal symptoms. But a common practice for me was drinking a bottle of wine in the evening hours during the week, and maybe one and a half bottles on a weekend night. It was a serious problem. And just as big of a problem, if not a bigger one, although not so easily identifiable as the substance abuse, was how I related to my romantic partners.

Relationship problems, along with addictions, are part and parcel of childhood trauma. (Although we don't have access to the intimate details of their lives, it is clear from their behavior that these Buddhist leaders also had problems developing healthy relationships.) My particular "attachment style," for those who know that term, was "avoidant."

The history of my major romantic relationships is dreadful. A trail strewn with tears. I was blessed with wonderful partners who offered their love, but I could not fully love in return because I didn't know how—or was unable. Most accurate: probably both. I was blocked, unable to be fully open and loving, unable to achieve true intimacy. Just unable. It wasn't that I would have known better if I had only read that one book, or anything like that. No; it wasn't possible for me to truly love anyone with my brain the way it was.

I had a great girlfriend in college and early graduate school, and we lived together for a while. I drove her away by not being able to love her fully. I later married a wonderful woman; we had a 16-year marriage and two lovely children whom we dearly loved and love. I broke that marriage, too. I subsequently met a delightful lady and we had a 13-year marriage, but she left me because of my drinking and unavailability to intimacy.

About this past, I have no self-blame, no guilt. Of course, I wish things could have been different. I do have great gratitude for their love. To all of them.

I have re-married again, to a truly sweet and lovely woman. I hope not to screw it up. Which brings me back to the storyline.

My wife and brother together pressured me to stop drinking alcohol and do something to make abstinence sustainable. Getting between a person and their addiction object is dangerous and tricky. The prospect terrified me, because this was my way to medicate my pain. However, I grudgingly said okay. I investigated AA, conventional psychotherapy, and FDA-approved drugs like Naltrexone, Acamprosate, and Disulfiram.

I also came across some reports of psychedelic compounds being used to treat addiction. Those stories were remarkable; they seemed too good to be true. They led me to Michael Pollan's bestselling book *How to Change Your Mind,* plus a lot of online material, including scientific literature. I decided to investigate further along that avenue, and found a licensed psychotherapist who, according to his published writing and his website, clearly knew how to handle psychedelic-assisted therapy. He was an "above ground" therapist, which means he didn't work directly with these substances which (unfortunately) currently are illegal in the United States. But he knew about psychedelics, how to use them, and what they are capable of.

I stopped drinking and began what you would call conventional talk therapy. I expressed why I was there (to maintain abstinence) and my therapist took my history. Over the months, he helped me use various tools like dream work, talk therapy, searching distant childhood memories, and investigating family history. Gradually, I got closer and closer to the source problem.

My symptoms included fear of being intimate with and trusting women. There was anger, too, about unmet affection. Without going into extensive detail about my early childhood, I came to learn that I had experienced threat of abandonment, actual abandonment, and emotional absence. Serious early childhood trauma. These behaviors are often passed from generation to generation, but knowing that doesn't help you if you are on the receiving end. Through this difficult but successful therapeutic work, I solved the mystery of my lifelong behavior; I solved my personal koan. This intellectual knowledge is the important first step on the road to healing, but it is not healing itself.

Talking about your past, to the extent that you can bring aspects up to the conscious level, and performing psychotherapeutic exercises both help you to process childhood trauma. But even with tools like focused hypnosis and EMDR therapy, it is slow work to effect healing. It can take years, I believe. I was interested in the possibility of accelerating my work with the assistance of the powerful medicines that I had been reading about in Pollan's book and elsewhere. The MAPS organization's successful FDA-approved Phase II treatment of PTSD with MDMA (3,4-methylenedioxymethamphetamine, or ecstasy) was especially intriguing, given that the trauma in my past was becoming more and more apparent as my therapy progressed. (There also is both historical and current FDA-approved research on addiction treatment using psilocybin and other strong medicines.)

While continuing my psychotherapy, and in conjunction with it, I engaged an underground psychotherapist who was willing to work with me using these strong medicines to treat my trauma (first MDMA, and then psilocybin). The MDMA journeys, conducted under this therapist's expert support and supervision, successfully uncovered and healed the bulk of the source of my pain and dysfunction.

Is my work healing my trauma completed? I believe it is mostly finished. It's hard to put a 100% label on this kind of thing, and I don't try to do so, but I bow deeply to my therapists and to the strong medicine which was used in a respectful and responsible manner. Just as I bow deeply to the Buddha statue on the altar, my teachers, and the person across from me. We're all together in this.

Is there a lesson here for all of us? Clearly, yes—at least in my mind, and hopefully for others, too. Nearly all of us have our own personal koan to solve. It is my recommendation that before any individuals are ordained or granted teaching privileges in any religion, they must first complete psychotherapy by a certified therapist. (Psychotherapists routinely must undergo therapy as part of their own training.) Healing work and spiritual training are a compelling combination.

Ideally, the therapists will not only be certified by the state, as now required, but they also will have special training in preparing clergy for their roles in society. Furthermore, they should be able to grant a therapeutic certification that clergy members need to obtain before they can be recognized by their particular religious order. Therapists would be experts in treating early childhood and other traumas, as well as a range of other psychological problems. They would look closely for obvious and not-so-obvious signs of addictive behavior in any form. We can also anticipate a time in the near future when powerful medicines are legally available to certified therapists, helping to make the healing more effective and efficient.

Can we foresee hindrances to this goal? Some religions will resist, believing that they know better or that their already-existing processes work. Evidence shows that this is not the case, however. Another hindrance will, of course, come from those individuals who, whether intentionally or unintentionally, resist treatment by not being honest and forthright with the therapist, and by not allowing themselves to be vulnerable – like a baby, like a little child. Traumas are often hidden from readily accessed memory, and working in a fully honest manner with the therapist is essential to reaching back in time. Without self-exploration and psychotherapy, abuse will continue to flourish in religious settings as unhealed trauma surfaces in extremely harmful ways.

Can meditation actually heal trauma after the experience of the trauma has been elevated into the conscious? That's debatable. I believe the answer probably is yes, although difficult, as long as the meditation focuses on the memories and feelings of the original trauma (and they are accessible), and not, for example, just on the breath or a mantra. But there is absolutely no question in my mind that skilled psychotherapy, in conjunction with powerful psychedelic medicines, comprise an effective and efficient healing combination for childhood trauma, resulting in the rebirth of the true self.

How is it that people in elevated spiritual positions can fall prey to their own demons? Because they don't realize their own traumatic history, and consequently, they haven't healed it. That's the koan that's now solved.

We already are vulnerable before God. I hope future clergy-in-training recognize the need to embrace their own vulnerability in the process of healing schisms often deeply shrouded in the unconscious. Let's shine divine light on this persistent problem and put an end to abuse.

LIBERATION

I surrender
Please love me

Some say
The meaning of life
Is authenticity

My vulnerability
And need for love
Is my authenticity

Then I can feel my pain,
Then I can feel your pain

Coming to peace
With our suffering
Is so beautiful

Then energy arises and
I can dance for people
With vitality and love.
Taking in their pain
Is how I am whole,
How I belong to the tribe

Dancing wildly,
Generating light,
Illuminating the source of pain –
The loss of self in childhood –
May I please help many heal

TASTY FOOD

"Termites! Everything is eating!"

So I said during a journey into pain, when the powerful earth medicine showed me the universal character of suffering.

The need to eat is everywhere. The need for food and the pain of hunger permeate this world. Even insects, like the termites in my vision, are voracious eaters. (I had a recent encounter with termites, and so this connection popped up in my journey.)

This is the prime character of life, this constant eating.

The opposite of pain is comfort and pleasure. During and after a good meal, sentient beings are comforted.

Humans are a special case, of course. Although we share the universal need to eat, we also have the unique ability to prepare our food with the intention of making it tasty.

"Tasty" is a delightful quality. You know it when you encounter it. The ability to judge food for its tastiness comes from innate knowledge. Tasty food represents safe and nourishing food. You don't need to have a lot of experience or take a special course to know if a food is tasty. And although it's true that some foods are quite tasty in their natural state—berries, for example—it is also true that humans create our own combinations of foods that are hugely varied and wonderfully tasty.

There are so many cuisines and recipes! So many cultures and regions and people creating their own tasty foods!

Recently, while driving around my neighborhood, I saw a bumper sticker on the back of a car. It had two lines of text. In big letters at the top, it said, "Love people." Underneath that, in smaller text, it said, "Cook them tasty food." (The sticker is supplied by a spice company, which includes it in its shipments.)

When I saw the bumper sticker, I thought, "What a great message!" I mean, Love people; cook them tasty food. That's beautiful. There's a connection, too, between the words:

TASTY ↔ LOVE

And it's not only a great message. Cooking tasty food also can be a kind of spiritual practice, something most of us can do. It just requires sincere effort and careful attention. That's really all it takes. You're not merely putting something out there to be consumed. If you're cooking tasty food, then you're making a deliberate, conscious effort to prepare it well. You have to care deeply about what you are providing, and, by extension, love the people you are serving (which can include yourself, too). The effort to make it right takes concentration, and it unquestionably is a form of practice. Cooking, therefore, is an opportunity to practice mindfulness in a creative and nourishing way.

The other thing about this kind of spiritual practice, cooking tasty food, is that it's got a great feedback mechanism. When you're attempting to prepare a delicious meal, you have to taste the food! And if you're tasting while cooking and you say, "Wow, yeah! This is tasty!" then you know you're doing it right. You don't have to wonder—*Am I doing this correctly?* or *Is this okay?* You know immediately. Plus, the people you serve give you feedback, too. They may say, "This is fantastic, delicious!" Or they may just wolf it down and then thank you for it.

You can even call this practice, this sincere effort to prepare and share tasty food, a Cathedral of Food.

When I think of love, deep caring, and dedicated spiritual practice, I also think of religions. Religions derive from different cultures and traditions, and they have different practices and teachings and beliefs, but they share something at their core. In fact, you might say religions are like types of foods—they have their own flavors and consistencies, so to speak, but they also have a common element: love.

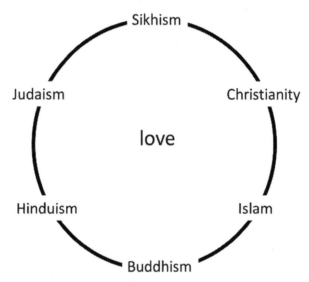

Although love is emphasized more clearly by some religions than by others, I would argue that it is the basis of all religions.

Mindful and caring preparation and sharing of tasty food is a spiritual practice and a practice of love for all religions and their followers. So let's take delight in preparing the tastiest food we can. In this way, we let love flow through us and into the hearts of those we feed.

Love people; cook them tasty food.

LEAF BLOWER MEDITATION

Or it could be a chain saw.
VERY loud. In my case
There were two. SO loud
And in perfect dissonance.
RoaAR roarrr ROARRRR
Difficult to write how jarring
Ragged and annoying the sound.
But you know, we've all been
Near the loud leaf blower.
In this case it started at seven
Just as I sat to meditate
And lasted one hour.
Often I thought: it must end soon;
How long can you leaf blow?
But it lasted and lasted.
I let it in, let it all in,
Let it soak into my core,
The irregular roar from outside.
Let it be just good practice.
But after so much of that
I shifted my meditation –
I contemplated suffering.
This roar being so trivial, but how
Loud and long the leaf blower of life
Blows for many, blowing
Burning sand in their face,
Blowing icy cold through clothes,
Blowing loss and loneliness into hearts.

May I take in and release the
Wind of their pain,
May I quiet that leaf blower noise.

SPIRITUAL REPORTER ON THE DIVINE LIGHT

Star date April 13, 2019

What do I know? What do I believe I know? What have I experienced?

I'm sitting on the couch at home, having just watched a snippet of a YouTube interview with Huston Smith, well-known authority on the world's religions. He spoke on the use of entheogens (psychoactive substances used for spiritual revelation and growth) and his experiences with them. Seven of them, he said. He inspired me to start writing. Thank you, Huston.

Earlier today, I was at a Zen Buddhist sesshin, a (one-day) retreat. My life and mind have been quite busy lately, bouncing around a lot, understandable because there's been a lot going on for me. But in the later part of the retreat, I began to settle down in my meditation and the light got to be quite bright, like the mid-day sun. (The light has been with me a long time now, one way or another.) Nowadays, I sometimes meditate with my eyes open, facing a blank wall, "wall gazing" style; and sometimes with them closed. Maybe half the period one way and the next half the other, or whatever I feel like that day. I can report that the light definitely doesn't depend on your eyelids!

It is truly wonderful to behold. I don't think there is a physical sensation to it, or at least I'm not recalling one. Maybe some subtle, uplifting feeling, with equanimity. But what is it? What is this light? Is it spiritual light, or some brain malfunction? Let's go with spiritual, divine light.

I believe it's not really like God saying hello, but rather just opening to what is always present. God, Buddha, Yahweh, Allah, the Lord, Jesus, the Source, or whatever name you prefer. It's what we are, not something "out there." Or at least I think that's the case. Funny thing about this spirituality work—nobody has "the answer," although many have opinions expressed as "the answer." But anyway, that's my interpretation, and it's certainly not a unique one. That is, not only is the light always there, but we are composed of it. We are the light.

That's today, Saturday. Now for the past, my spiritual past.

Growing up, I always was interested in religion. My mother was Presbyterian and my father Jewish. I sometimes went to church with my mom, although Christianity didn't stick with me. I always appreciated having parents from two different traditions; it gave me a little stereovision and a lack of attachment to any one religion.

In the early 1970s, spirituality was in the air. I took an eastern religions class in college, at Columbia University; they had an excellent East Asian studies library that I liked to wander around in. One day, seemingly at random, I pulled from the shelf a book written by the Buddhist teacher Nagarjuna (translated into English, of course). I opened it up somewhere in the middle and began to read. I think I only read a few pages; then I closed the book and decided I was a Buddhist. That's how it happened.

It's not like I had never heard about Buddhism before. I know I had read some other things, like an Alan Watts book. Huston Smith's *The World's Religions* was on our syllabus, as was an overview work on Buddhism. Although I don't recall what I read in Nagarjuna's book, it must have been a zinger as it sealed the deal. Just made sense to me.

Around this time, the early- and mid-1970s, like many other people, I had several experiences with peyote, psilocybin mushrooms, and LSD. I approached these plant and synthetic medicines as entheogens, substances to help spiritual awakening, spiritual understanding. What is this world? How did I get here? Why am I in this body? What is consciousness?

I read a couple of Carlos Castaneda's books, and they got me interested in peyote. The peyote trips were the most rewarding for me and constituted most of my experiences. I know there was light I could see in the trips, a brightness to everything. A brightness to the world. There was a certain satisfaction, a relaxation into nature, an intuitive, knowing comfort. These journeys were all done with eyes open, and usually, although not always, outside in nature.

I would say that I wasn't mature enough, or developed enough, to achieve the full benefits of these trips. Integration into my life was weak at best. Certainly, there was no conscious integration, no sense of deep self-examination, and thus, no deep healing. I guess you might call them spiritual appetizers. There was also no meditation practice to support the experience—if that's the right thing to say. I think that has validity. And there was absolutely no psychotherapy directed to understanding my personal history and dysfunctions. There was nothing like the careful integration after journeys that I have experienced with the help of my therapist-guide in my recent work. Maybe you could sum up my early experiences with the word "immature." Not a total waste. Not at all. Some roots were planted. But perhaps this recounting of my initial exploration will serve as a word of caution to any younger readers.

The last time I employed an entheogen during that span of my life was in graduate school, probably about 1976. I did enjoy marijuana a lot; too much, actually—this was part of my addictive behavior.

Back to my spiritual "practice." Several Zen books later, I finally got around to practicing sitting meditation, zazen. It took me awhile because meditation, or at least Zen meditation, seemed so scary. But it was 1975 and I was in graduate school at Berkeley, and I was introduced to Seung Sahn, a Korean Jogye Zen teacher. He was very charismatic, and he liked to use koans, zazen, and chanting. Chanting was a big thing for him. He was a terrific chanter and he gave me a love for it, showed how it could be valuable even though I don't get a chance to do much of it at my local Zen center.

I took lay ordination with Seung Sahn in 1977. My dharma name is Dao Zhen; it's Chinese, translated as True Way. As part of his ritual, Seung Sahn made a little burn on the initiate's skin, inside their left forearm. I have a 6-mm-diameter white circle still. He said it symbolized burning away karma. It's a reminder, certainly.

Around that time, I discovered that there was a Soto Zen Buddhist center just a couple blocks from where I lived. I could roll out of bed and be there for morning meditation. The teacher, Mel Weitsman, was friendly, as I recall. An encouraging, warm man.

I graduated from Berkeley with my Ph.D. in chemistry, and left for a post-doc on the east coast at MIT. I didn't really enjoy that; I missed California. I did fall into a fun living situation, and I still have a close friend from the large shared house where I lived. During that time, though, I mostly dropped my meditation practice. Not exactly sure why. Certainly, I was busy with my research, and I was probably aligning with career interests and worries. Becoming more "worldly."

That worldliness and lack of a solid meditation practice continued after I moved back to California and took a job, got married, and had my first child. That is, until my father's death on the last day of 1985. I was sad, but really, the only strong outpouring of sadness, of grief, was the moment I dropped dirt onto his casket. After that, there was a strange calm, contrary to the grieving one might expect. This is what brought me back into Zen practice in early 1986. It's difficult to make logical sense of that—calmness rather than distress driving me back to spiritual practice—but that was my experience. Maybe a sense something was missing.

Then, in February of 1986, I looked in the yellow pages (yes, we had them and used them!) and found the local Zen center near me. I began practice, attended quite regularly, and was an active member of the sangha. I brought my two kids there, too, to dharma school and the playground.

I was an ardent seeker by this time. I wondered especially about visual effects and whether they were spiritually significant—whether they indicated getting close to spiritual enlightenment. For example, I contemplated what happens when you put temporary pressure on your optic nerve, like when you cough too hard or get bumped in the head and "see stars." I also had some mild visual "floaters" that I was interested in. Laughable, now; I know. My teacher batted away my mistaken notions.

My meditation was deepening, however, and around 1988 or 1989, during zazen, I started to see a luminous sort of cloud forming and slowly changing shape—it's hard to describe exactly—gently undulating, expanding, and contracting, with a moving, fine structure. I described this to my teacher one day and he said, "Yes, that's it," and added, "Don't worry if it doesn't appear at every sitting." As my practice continued, I observed this luminous cloud vision during almost every meditation period. It was becoming routine, yet lovely, calming, even nurturing to my psyche.

Then in 1998, I separated from my first wife and got divorced. I felt greatly embarrassed and ashamed by my separation—so much, in fact, that I stopped going to the Zen center. Plus, I'd developed a level of complacency based on my experience with the luminous cloud. I believed that I had reached some sort of spiritual height, even though it looks more now like just a plateau. This hiatus continued for the next 12 years.

During that break, my practice was weak, and I meditated inconsistently. It is hard however, to turn off mindfulness once you've been practicing for a long time, and a certain degree of mindfulness undoubtedly was part of my daily life. Alcohol kept me sedated, and the worldliness of work and life stuff kept me busy and away from spiritual practice—although to be fair, none of those distractions had gone away when I came back to Zen.

For some reason, I decided to return to my practice in earnest. Probably just a feeling that the clock was ticking. It was around 2010. I felt I was stuck in a rut, asleep at the wheel; and I still yearned for a deeper spiritual understanding that somehow I knew I was missing. The embarrassment of my first marriage ending in divorce was fading from my psyche.

Soon after, I started attending the local Zen center and re-started a consistent meditation practice. I decided I should double my efforts, so to speak, with two or sometimes three sitting periods each day, usually at home. Time was slipping away, and being 60 years old, I felt I needed to get on with a more intense practice if I ever was going to deepen my understanding.

After about 5 months (perhaps I should have kept a journal), one morning while meditating, I experienced a great flash of light. It lasted only a second or two. It was almost like a mandala with colors, but it was so brief, I'm not sure I could describe it accurately. It seemed to wash over me as it disappeared. I sensed immediately that something had changed, that this was significant, although I wasn't sure what exactly had just happened.

Then, about two weeks later while I was in the zendo in meditation, this great flash happened again. It perhaps was even more intense, if that were possible. And then it was over. Nothing like it since, but from then on, spiritual light seems to be pervasive even when I am not meditating. Usually there is a dim luminescence everywhere if I look for it, especially when I'm not in bright sunlight. While in meditation, a more (although not completely) uniform, brighter light can come and go. This has a somewhat different and more encompassing character than the luminous cloud I described earlier.

I was 61 when this happened. I continued with my Zen meditation practice in the intervening six years and enjoyed what I take to be sitting in the spiritual light. My life otherwise wasn't so great, though, with addiction and relationship issues. This brings me to close to the present day, to just a few months ago. After significant psychotherapy to help heal my early childhood trauma, I undertook my first MDMA journey. MDMA is usually considered an empathogen, not an entheogen; that is, it is not prone to cause a spiritual experience. However, spiritual experiences are occasionally reported. In my case, I experienced a wonderful spiritual event.

What I remember was suddenly being totally surrounded by a most powerful and wonderful golden light. There was a slight texture to it, like a shimmering. Words cannot capture the experience. There was no "me," no body, no Chris, no absence-of-Chris—just this awesome, powerful golden light everywhere. I don't remember traveling there or undergoing some transition to get there. I was just there. I somehow became one with the golden light, and its character was LOVE. Love and nothing but love. The powerful shimmering light was everywhere, without end. And I knew this is eternal life. This is our home.

I don't know if my years of meditation helped make this spiritual and healing experience happen, but I do know the MDMA played a major role, a role of transformation.

Days after that journey, I recall sitting zazen in the Zendo, like at sesshin today, and the light was brighter still. Very bright. Truly wonderful. Words cannot capture it.

I mentioned this positive change in my meditation to my therapist, who practices Vipassana. He said, "It sounds like you removed a block." Makes sense, I suppose.

In a few days, I will have a psilocybin mushroom medicine experience with my trusted guide, the first since I was in my twenties. I will report on that next, as best I can. Who knows where this journey will take me, but I feel guided by the divine light. I'm grateful to experience it, grateful that it has grown bright. Perhaps it is lighting my way home.

The Mystery is a mystery. Yet it is our home.

Please come in.

REVELATION

I'm not afraid to die
Because I feel loved.
I'm not afraid to die
Having seen eternal life.
Bathed in golden light,
Shimmering, powerful,
Great furnace of love,
All around, without end.

I couldn't see it 'til now
For all my hurts and longings.
Although a luminous sea
Appeared before
Connecting you and me,
I sensed there must be more.

I'm thankful for the guides,
Explorers, returners
Who came bearing compassion.
They brought the jewel gift
For the seekers, walking, wandering,
Searching to touch the real.
Healing their confused hurt
So they too could
Bathe in the golden light
Of God's love.

THREE COMMON PROBLEMS

Although meditation is not a requirement to healing with psychedelics under the care of a well-trained and caring therapist-guide, mindfulness meditation can be extremely helpful, and is encouraged. So... Why meditate? That's an important and lovely subject in and of itself. Meditation **increases** awareness, focus, happiness, physical health, and spiritual insight. It **decreases** stress, constant worry, and distraction.

Meditation can be difficult, however. It generally takes time for meditation to have a demonstrable effect. Meditation also can be frustrating if your mind doesn't do what you want it to, which is usually the case. Consequently, it is easy to drop the practice.

I've been practicing meditation for 30 years. Most of my meditation has been in the Zen style, known as zazen, but I also have experience with Vipassana or Insight meditation, as well as mantra meditation like "Transcendental Meditation." (I'll sometimes use the term "zazen," which translates to "sitting meditation," to refer to all these methods.) Over the decades,

I've identified three common obstacles to meditation. Thankfully, these obstacles all are possible to overcome. I hope these considerations will be helpful to some.

Problem 1: Monkey Mind

Let's begin with how we deal with the thoughts that arise during meditation. This mental activity is referred to as mind-wandering, being distracted, the spontaneous arising of thoughts, and, metaphorically, monkey mind—when our thoughts are constantly swinging from branch to branch. It's a normal human phenomenon. That's what our mind does. Some of us have more of this mind-wandering than others, which may reflect our physiology as well as personal history (trauma history, personality traits, etc.). But we all have wandering minds to some degree; indeed, generally to a very significant degree.

The "goal" for some meditative techniques is to "quiet" the mind; that is, significantly reduce this mind-wandering through mindfulness techniques. Sometimes, people set a goal of having an "empty mind," with no thinking whatsoever. Too much can be made of this, however, as if you are a meditation athlete and need to complete a 40-minute session with fewer than 4 mind-wanderings in order to make the team (strain to make it zero, perfectionists!). This mindset originates in the mistaken idea that if only you can stop your mind, the heavens will open, enlightenment will blossom, and you will enter the blissful state of nirvana. Stop thinking that! (Smiley face.) Instead, a good starting point is... relax. Even accomplished, deep meditators still have some mind-wandering. In fact, you're wonderful even if you are a beginner and your monkey mind is going a mile a minute!

At the same time, it's important to acknowledge that meditation can indeed help quiet the mind—or, as some teachers put it, decrease the tyranny of the mind. What is tyranny of the mind? It's when our thoughts and feelings dominate us in an unwelcome and uncontrolled fashion, when our mind controls us and not the other way around. We allow the mind to tyrannize us when we identify our self, our ego, with every thought and feeling. Suffering is the predictable consequence. The Buddhist principle of "nonattachment" counters this mistaken equation of thought with self.

It's important to note that the principle of nonattachment is sometimes misunderstood, which then can cause us to deny our feelings. This leads to the "spiritual bypassing" of psychological wounds and the avoidance of healing work. In these cases, nonattachment is a misapplied and even dangerous concept. However, when applied with honest self-awareness and love, nonattachment can guide us into a relaxed and attentive meditation. This, in turn, can help us quiet our minds, so we're not out of control, not being tyrannized.

How? Here we go.

In Zen and other Buddhist traditions, the primary meditation techniques take what psychologists call focused attention (FA) or open monitoring (OM) approaches. In OM, also called shikantaza (a Chinese term for "just sitting"), one mindfully focuses on mind-body contents (consciousness) without trying to focus on or control any one of them in particular. This is a practice of pure awareness of the present moment. In contrast, Zen beginners often use the FA approach, focusing, for example, on the breath. When I first received zazen instruction, I was told to count my breath from one to ten, and then start again at one. It was a rare event when I made it to ten! And when I say "rare," I am not exaggerating. I expect some readers will identify with that.

And here we see the core of problem #1. You're sitting there after yet another session of mind-wandering, and you start thinking, "Damn! I've been meditating for quite a while now, and I still keep getting carried away by my thoughts." And you go back to your breath, and immediately engage in another five-minute wandering trip, whereupon you say to yourself, "Shit! I'm not getting anywhere!" Etc. Etc. Etc. Etc. Etc. Etc. Etc. Etc. Etc. Etc.

Almost all meditation instructors will tell you not to worry about your mind-wandering—it's normal—and to just return to your breath over and over again. Problem #1 is many (most?) of us ignore that gentle instruction and berate ourselves anyway. Why is that?

There are many reasons we engage in excessive self-criticism. Being raised by parents who did not make us feel unconditionally valued and loved can create an unconscious need to achieve and be successful, in order to "win" their love as adults. Hence, if we perceive we're not succeeding, this then can create an anxious need to "fix" the problem. Severe childhood trauma, or Adverse Childhood Experiences, also can create a "false self," rendering us vulnerable to self-criticism (see "A Public Service Announcement").

I suggest that the meditator's self-critical reaction to wandering thoughts is more common among Zen students than Vipassana students. This is due to the difference between the cultures of the two meditation schools. Vipassana generally focuses more intently on the problem of self-criticism, and Vipassana also has a much stronger tradition of teaching loving kindness for oneself (as well as for others). Zen, on the other hand, has developed a hard-edged attitude of try harder, do it better, do it longer, don't move, and be correct. Although lip service is given to self-compassion, Zen is not a self-compassionate culture. Self-compassion is not in its marrow. That's my experience anyway.

Back to the obstacle itself. The problem is not actually the mind wandering; it's the self-critical reaction to mind wandering. Not only is this a needless infliction of pain, self-criticism adds fuel to the fire by energizing the mind-wandering. And it's a significant discouragement to practice, too. All bad. So, what to do?

I'm sure many teachers have given gentle guidance on how to handle this problem. I'm going to paraphrase a talk I heard by Vipassana teacher James Baraz, who suggested a variety of loving approaches responding to your wandering mind. You can use one approach one day and another on a different day.

The first approach is to begin cultivating a heart of self-love, self-forgiveness, and self-compassion. Instead of blaming yourself, integrate lovingkindness meditation into your practice. Specifically, every time you realize your mind is wandering, forgive yourself and come back, bringing loving understanding of these crazy minds of ours.

Another approach is to celebrate! I love this one. "Yeah! I just came back! That's what minds do!"

Baraz's third suggestion is to lovingly remind yourself that you are making a sincere effort. The Dali Lama teaches, "My sincere effort is my great protection." You're wonderful! You're making a sincere effort! How beautiful you are! There's nothing to be concerned about.

You also can remember the emptiness of those wandering thoughts. They come from nothing and go nowhere. This realization can be freeing.

And finally, Baraz urges us to take delight in the great awareness of our minds—it's amazing that we can recognize those thoughts and feelings.

I also offer a few additional techniques that you can apply to mind-wandering during zazen. Oftentimes, when we realize we have been lost in thought, we rush back to our breath (or another object of focus), dropping the subject of our mind-wandering like a hot potato. Please don't rush. Take at least a couple of seconds to clearly note, without judgment, the content of your wandering thoughts or the feelings that arose. This will help you better understand yourself and unwind some of the mental energy associated with those thoughts and feelings. Were you thinking, remembering, restless, itchy? If you find there is a common pattern to your wandering, you can describe it in a little more detail. Were you thinking about work, or thinking about your partner, or fantasizing, or rehearsing? Finding a pattern will help illuminate what your mind is inclining toward. To some extent, there is value in the saying: "If you can name it, you can tame it." But don't get into a discursive analysis of your wanderings. Just calmly return to your object of focus, like your breath, without judging or comparing.

Sometimes, these wandering thoughts and associated feelings have little or no emotional energy associated with them. For example, they may be about your shopping list—"I have to remember to pick up bread." But other times, they are associated with a great deal of emotional energy. You may be reflecting on a heated disagreement with your romantic partner or boss, or grieving the loss of a loved one. When you experience strong feelings like sadness, longing, grief, anxiety, anger, or joy, don't return directly to the breath. Instead, replace the breath with these feelings as the object of your focused attention. Without judging, trying to make the feeling go away, or engaging in discursive thought, observe the feeling with full attention. Where in the body are you having these feelings, and with what sensations? Allow yourself to feel and investigate any strong emotion that arises, whether pleasant or unpleasant. Mindfulness of your feelings is as important as mindfulness of your breath. It's much healthier to be in touch with your feelings than to deny or bury them. Allowing yourself to feel "negative" feelings can help heal the source of the pain.

Sometimes, focusing attention on a difficult feeling will reveal a hidden underlying cause. This can be extremely therapeutic. Be curious about your mind. What's really going on? Become aware of your psychological wounds, and even uncover unconscious issues. If, like so many of us, you have long-standing problems such as substance abuse, depression, anxiety, or anger, a psychotherapist may help you identify and work on their buried causes.

On the other hand, recognize that not all mind-wandering is negative. If you are distracted by feelings of happiness and joy, dwelling on them will help them stay in your heart.

So take some time to feel and investigate your emotions. Don't rush back to your breath. You may want to take only 20 seconds, but 10 or 20 minutes or even the whole period is okay, too, if that feels right. When the intensity of the feeling begins to fade, that's a good time to return to your breath. This is not a race. It's a journey to understand and heal ourselves. Our spiritual nature will appear by itself, all by itself.

Problem 2: Apprehension

How do we approach the meditation period? How are we feeling in the hours and days before a meditation retreat, or in the minutes and seconds before sitting down? Often, we approach the impending meditation period or retreat with dread, apprehension, or even fear. Doubt and confusion also can be present. What's going on here? What is this about?

Several different mindsets can lead to this apprehension. You may have an expectation that pain and discomfort are imminent. You may be anxious about whether you will need to move during the meditation period. You might worry about feeling shame or embarrassment if you do move (Zen peer pressure!), even if someone tells you it's okay to move (but not too much!). There may be self-doubt, especially before a retreat—Can I do this? Am I capable?

Then there's the bugaboo of dreading more of the same mind-wandering. If you find that meditation after meditation is 90% mind-wandering, it can wear on you if you're not careful. If you believe you aren't "getting anywhere" (where are you going?), that can be a hindrance. A feeling of failure certainly can be discouraging, and as you approach the cushion, understandably, apprehension can arise. And repeated apprehension can lead to a break in your practice.

Well, a lot of life is about choice and attitude. What if you approach your cushion thinking... This is like sitting in my mother's (or Buddha's) lap while she holds me and loves me.

Whether my mind wanders or not, or whether my knee hurts or not, or whether I feel focused or not, this is the place where I have 100% permission to express my pure and wonderful self. No one can take that away from me. (And don't let anyone try.)

800 years ago, Dogen (the Soto Zen founder) wrote that you should go to zazen like "your hair is on fire." I have another suggestion. How about you go to zazen like you are about to receive the biggest, warmest, most loving hug? Like you are about to receive the gift of life, and gratitude washes all over you? Every moment, every breath is the gift of life. Even your wandering thoughts are beautiful. And don't worry; things will settle down over time.

Perhaps you find this easier said than done. Perhaps you have every intention of approaching your cushion or your retreat like you are going home, going to that safe and loving home—but there still is some apprehension. If that is the case, investigate that feeling; be curious about it. Why is it arising? Where do you feel it in your body? Take the opportunity to make this investigation part of your meditation. Examine it closely; observe it without judgment. You will probably find that the feeling dissipates, but don't force it. Be gentle with any feeling of apprehension. Let it express itself fully, so you have an opportunity to gain wisdom about it and hopefully heal its source.

A word or two about moving during zazen. Please move. Pretty please with sugar on it, feel free to move. Am I kidding? No, siree. If you are made of wood or stone, you shouldn't move. Absolutely, don't move if you're a branch or a pebble. Stay perfectly still. But you aren't made of wood or stone. So, it's okay to move. Zazen is not an endurance contest. Its purpose is not to produce pain. It's true that fidgeting during zazen or any meditation method will not serve you. So work at not fidgeting, if that's an issue. And not moving at the first sign of discomfort is good mindfulness practice for observing and not reacting. In time, it gets easier and easier to sit still for longer periods. But when you feel you need to move, please move. Try to do so quietly, and know a good rest position, if that's what you need. Everyone should learn a good rest position. As your meditation practice deepens, you will naturally sit still for longer periods.

Now when you approach your cushion, I pray you see it as your place of rest (with good posture to keep you comfortable and stable). Rest in the arms of Buddha, of God, of Mother Earth, of the ancestors who love you, of your loved ones now. Come home; be comforted because now you are home.

Problem 3: Zen Sickness

The third problem (especially for Zen students) is quite different, and although it's not as common as the other two, I don't think it's rare. It tends to afflict the real zealots in the group (count me as a former member). The problem is believing the world is not real. Indeed, the idea that we cannot trust our senses is embedded in Zen history and literature. It is a serious problem, sometimes referred to as "Zen sickness."

That might sound odd to a lot of us, but the misunderstanding actually comes out of Buddhist literature. For example, a stanza from the influential Diamond Sutra reads:

> *As a lamp, a cataract, a star in space*
> *an illusion, a dewdrop, a bubble*
> *a dream, a cloud, a flash of lightning*
> *view all created things like this*
>
> *(Trans. Red Pine)*

When people view the world as an illusion, a bubble, or a dream, they can easily come to believe that the world is not real. If they reflect on words like "emptiness" and "no-thing" or "nothingness," they also might get this idea.

In one koan, the student reports to the teacher that all he sees and feels is not real. The master then whacks him with his staff and asks, "Was that real or unreal?" In the Zen poem "Faith Mind" by the third patriarch of Chinese Zen, Sengstan, it says:

> *If you wish to move in the One Way*
> *Do not dislike even the world of senses and ideas.*
> *Indeed, to accept them fully*
> *Is identical with true Enlightenment.*
>
> *(Trans. Richard Clarke)*

So the message to anyone doubting is: Yes, the world is real. For all its imperfections, it is a marvelous place. It's where we live.

Conclusion

Meditation is an opportunity to learn about ourselves, come to peace with our perceived imperfections, and realize our inherent beauty and goodness. Given our personal histories, however, we have a tendency to trip ourselves along this journey of growth. We frequently hinder our own development, and then give up. Recognizing common obstacles that we place before ourselves can help us overcome them and realize the fruits of meditation. May your path to self-knowledge be decorated with the brightest jewels of the universe.

WORDS

Words are like stones
You skip on a pond
Or throw and hurt people
Or build a wide path

Words are like fingers
That strum the guitar
Or grasp and squeeze tight
Or gently caress

Words are like water
You dive in to cool
Or drift out to sea
Or quench a great thirst

Words are like songs
You sing to express
A pain in your heart
You heal with pure love

MORE WORDS

Words can persuade, dissuade,
Discourage, encourage,
Reveal, conceal,
Be precious and righteous,
Dirty and disgusting,
Darken or brighten,
Say you hate or love.
They can do so much!

What can't they do?
They can't make you or me,
Can't make the sun shine,
Can't touch or kiss, or
Color the flower's petals.

SPIRITUAL REPORTER ON THE CELESTIAL WASHING MACHINE - PART 1

Star date April 20, 2019

I'm writing this two nights after my first psilocybin mushroom journey in roughly 40 years. Let's count this as a new experience, although it did bring back some memories. Yes, the sacred mushroom journey is a Celestial Washing Machine. It cleans you if you're ready, and you get tossed around in the process.

How to unpack this? I don't think it will be too easy. First of all, two days later is still early to be recording this. The writing will probably have to continue for a few days. Reporting on the evening of the journey day would just be silly, if not impossible. So that's one thing to share, a common bit of wisdom that everyone on a similar path should know. When you're using psilocybin mushrooms (and probably ayahuasca or peyote), don't try to make sense of it right away. Certainly not on the same day. Just rest. In fact, my initial thoughts when coming down from the journey were I don't think I want to do this again and I don't know if I learned anything. Both of these assessments had changed by the next day.

Throughout the journey, I sometimes spoke out loud and my guide wrote down my words; much of this essay is based on his recordings. Overall, however, I didn't say much, especially considering the journey lasted several hours. There was a lot of mental processing that didn't get translated into words.

I began ingesting about 10:15 AM. But I don't want to get ahead of myself. Some words are warranted on set and setting and the mechanics of entering the Celestial Washing Machine.

First, on the set and setting. I loved our altar. We had everything covered. I brought a small Buddha statue, a little footed brass cup for water, and a small, smooth, black river stone (water and earth). There was dried sage already on the altar, a few American and Mexican Indian objects, some with feathers, and a couple other objects of unknown origin. We lit a Virgin Mary candle. A large, beautifully carved wooden Buddha rested on a nearby stand. My Intentions were written on a piece of paper and placed on the altar.

In my previous MDMA journeys, I had specific psychological healing tasks to work on. I brought childhood photos of myself and my family to help focus on these tasks. This time, however, my intentions were more general:

Surrender and go with the journey.
Let down my defenses, be fully open and
nonjudgmental with Nancy [my wife] and everyone.
Whatever needs to be taught and healed, let it please
arise.

Surrender to the source. May I be released from
grasping and clinging.
May my heart be filled with love for all.

My guide said a beautiful prayer to implore teaching and healing by the plant medicine. He lit a bundle of dried sage and blew out the flame so the sage would emit smoke, which we used in a cleansing ceremonial fashion. Then, he handed me a small plate holding dried psilocybin mushrooms with a dribble of honey on the side. There was a cup of water to drink from, too.

He took a walk, leaving me alone to eat the mushrooms. My instructions were to use a Native Mexican traditional technique, using only my front teeth to bite the mushrooms into little pieces, rolling them around in my mouth until it felt good to swallow. I ate very slowly, letting the mushrooms sit in my mouth for a long time. I think it must have taken at least twenty minutes to eat the 3.5 grams. By allowing much of the psilocybin to be absorbed through my mouth, the onset of its effects was quick. I began to feel the mushrooms essentially as soon as I was done eating.

Because of the rapid onset and relatively rapid decline of the medicine (the most intense part of the journey only lasted a relatively short 3 or 4 hours), the peak concentration of psilocybin in my system was probably higher than if I had gulped down the mushrooms into my stomach. Plus, scientific literature reports a considerably lower concentration of monoamine oxidase (MAO) enzymes (which deactivate a fraction of the psilocybin molecules) in the mouth cavity, where much of the medicine was absorbed, versus in the small intestine. So, I suspect the 3.5 grams I consumed in this manner gave me a jolt equivalent to a bigger dose swallowed quickly into the stomach. I can't be quantitative about that; it would be interesting to perform a pharmacokinetic study comparing the ingestion approaches. But I'm digressing!

After eating the mushrooms, I lay down on the thin mattress on the floor, covered myself with a blanket, and put on eye shades. This journey was in the dark, for introspection, like the other journeys I took. Soon after I finished the mushrooms, my guide returned and began playing recorded music. He is an expert in music selection, which is an important aid for the spiritual journey.

Now for the journey itself. A journey of cleaning, insight, and opening to love. A journey of healing.

Before I began, I wondered if I would be taken immediately to the field of divine light that I experienced on my first MDMA journey and during meditation. Instead, I found myself in the Washing Machine and it rapidly became intense. I'm not sure how to describe what it's like when the Celestial Washing Machine gets going, but I knew I had to let go and go with the journey, trust the journey.

The first thing I said out loud was *Kneel to Nancy.* I realized that it would be appropriate, and hopefully beneficial for both of us, for me to apologize to my wife on my knees—apologizing for the pain I caused her, especially while in the midst of my addictive behavior. What behavior? Seeking comfort from alcohol and sex, avoiding intimacy, lack of trust, judgmentalism, focusing on what I perceived as her (and others') faults while considering myself superior, becoming distant when conflict arose, and repressing emotions.

Sounds worth apologizing for, doesn't it? It's not that I haven't done some apologizing already, but kneeling while making a wholehearted apology struck me as cleansing and releasing. The plant medicine was teaching me to surrender my pride and admit my mistakes with love and without reservation. (And so I have done.)

The Celestial Washing Machine was just starting, however. My next statement was *I don't want to eat meat anymore.* I was feeling compassion for all animals and was repulsed at the notion of killing and eating them. Although I have been a vegetarian off and on throughout my life, I haven't been one recently. I am now more inclined to practice vegetarianism. I do have a conflict, in that my wife very much enjoys meat dishes and I am trying to be more, not less, aligned with her in our daily life. This is something I am still trying to come to grips with when we share a common meal. If we are eating out, I chose a vegetarian option.

Next, I told my guide *My heart is getting bigger*. Many times during the journey through the Machine, while lying on my back, I placed my hands over my heart and then spread my arms out wide in an "open, open, open" motion. There was great love coursing through me.

The mushroom medicine was opening my heart in an amazing way. I also told my guide I'm learning, which meant, I believe, that I was learning how to more completely open my heart to love.

This led to my saying, in tears, *I release you; I release you.* This meant that I released my wife and everyone else from the 'old Chris,' who did not just have addiction problems (the obvious manifestation), but also had problems relating to people in a selfless manner. For me to release others signified letting go and opening up to love in the most profound sense. In true love, there is no attachment. There are no requirements laid out, consciously or unconsciously; no bargains to be had. No strings attached. Just unconditional love.

Further on in the journey, I said *Letting everything go through me*. This referred to taking in the suffering of people I know and the suffering of the world. It is a Bodhisattva effort: accepting others' suffering in order to relieve it, and doing so in a way that is healthy and sustainable.

The Celestial Washing Machine was cleaning me and teaching me. What more could there be? It was all so amazing!

But there was indeed more, and this is where God stepped in, so to speak. I was overcome with the most incredible sense of JOY I have ever felt. It had to be DIVINE JOY, no doubt about it. Like all of us, I've had moments of great happiness and joy in my life: when my two children were born, and during other terrific events—a big career success, wonderful love making, my team winning the World Series, and so on. But nothing on this scale. Nothing, nothing, nothing like it.

I exclaimed *I can feel joy! Joy can come back; joy can come back!*

Why did I say, "Come back"? I can't really remember for sure, but believe I was recognizing a place where I had been before, long ago. Childhood? Before I was born? I don't know! But in any event, that's what came out of my mouth, and I'm sure I said it for a reason.

Clearly, part of my work now is to cultivate this divine joy. Not with the idea of getting something, but in order to be one with God, opening my heart to her or it. Joy is not external, but rather, always present; it flows through us. That's my understanding, anyway, and I think it was no accident that this divine joy followed my cry *Letting everything go through me.*

The later part of my journey had a different aspect. I was slowly beginning to descend from the most intense part. I sat up and removed my eyeshades. The medicine was still strong and it continued to provide teaching and healing, although it took a couple days for everything to clarify for me. Sometimes things seem jumbled in the Celestial Washing Machine, but it takes you where you need to go.

In this segment of the journey, I was thrust into a difficult emotional space where I was forced to confront—and ultimately be healed from—more early childhood trauma that I had not realized was present. There was a thought-laden aspect to this part. That is, I was aware of lots of thinking, unlike earlier in the journey, and the thinking felt burdensome. Around this time, my guide was playing beautiful and powerful Tibetan chanting. The chanter had that deep, resonant voice. I can't say how it influenced my journey or if it was a prompt for what came up, but it was perfect. The chanting conjured memories of my first Zen teacher, the late Seung Sahn, who was a big believer in chanting and a great chanter himself. I said *My teacher liked to chant*. I thought about my other Zen teachers, too. I realized I carried considerable tension about them. There was a history of attraction, respect, a desire to know what they knew (or what I thought/wished/hoped they knew). But there also was an aversion associated with distrust. I could not escape my thoughts during this part of my journey, the confusion, the push-pull.

I told my guide, with respect to his own training, "You must have had good guides." As soon as those words left my lips, I burst into a torrent of crying, uncontrollable crying with great tears. My guide stroked the hair on my head, comforting me, and within a few seconds, this big crying spell stopped. What was that about? What prompted it? Where did it come from?

It wasn't until the next day that I realized there was only one other time in my adult life when I cried like that. It was the very moment, 33 years ago, when I dropped dirt onto my father's casket. And suddenly, all became clear, the Celestial Washing Machine's teaching and healing.

Up until then, my father had played only a minor role in the work of healing my childhood trauma. Yet he was one of my two parents! And the father is an archetype, an authority figure and teacher. How could I have mostly missed him in my therapy? In this moment, I realized that my father had largely been absent during my childhood as well, and this absence fed another kind of childhood trauma.

The teaching? First, I learned that I have had deep-seated psychological confusion from wanting a present, loving father and teacher. Because I did not receive this love from my biological father, I have been attracted to Zen teachers as substitutes. However, this attraction has come with distrust, based on my experience of not being able to count on my father.

This realization has also helped clarify that learning is up to me, that I must trust myself. I simply need to be authentic. As Buddha reportedly said on his death bed, "Be a light unto yourself." I take this lesson to heart and have given up my interest in Zen priests, although I understand the role of clergy and I respect when their role is performed well.

The healing? I have finally buried my father.

I'm capable myself. I am the light. I am the wisdom. Just like you.

What an incredible journey in the Celestial Washing Machine! The places this medicine took me, the lessons, cleaning and healing it helped me with. We only need to open our hearts to love, to let the divine shine through and come home to ourselves.

Joy be with you! Praise be to Allah! Glory to God! Thanks to the Creator!

LETTER TO MY FATHER

Dear Dad,

Thank you for bringing me into this world. Thank you for working hard to provide for our family so that we had plenty of food and clothing, and a comfortable house to live in. Thank you for providing for my college education.

When I was a little kid, I didn't have a picture of what a loving and present father would be like, what a teaching father would be like. Little kids just know what's around them. They don't have abstract models to measure from.

My memory of my childhood was that you weren't around a lot. You worked long hours and you were pretty unhappy when you were home. And you could be stern. I'm sure that wasn't always the case, but it was, I think, mostly the case.

I only have one memory of you running, and that was to fly a kite for the three of us boys. I don't think it went up. I don't remember playing games or sports with you. I don't remember hiking with you.

I don't remember intellectual conversations with you, conversations that would nurture and encourage my growth.

When I was a teenager, I would go over to my friend Rob's house and we would have deep discussions with his dad. That was an eye-opening experience for me.

I developed my academic strengths as a way to garner your love and attention. I had to do this largely on my own, with some help from teachers. You became very proud of me, but only when I started earning high scores in school.

You grew up without a lot of money and you lived through the Depression, so making money and having a measure of social status was important to you. You worked toward that; you worked harder on that than on nurturing my feelings or making me feel wanted. I pretty much grew up without you.

All in all, our relationship was not great. You showed some heart. You relished your grandkids. I know you had it in you. But during my childhood, you were covered in unhappiness too much of the time. I'm sorry that you were dealt wounds in your life and didn't know how to heal from and grow past them.

I'm fortunate to have found a different path, although it hasn't been an easy one for me. Is it for anyone? Despite my own hurts, and even though I, too, had to work hard, I made a real effort to be present with my two children when they were young; and I still give them time and love. If they have children, I hope they do even better than I did in raising them. In some ways—ironically, perhaps; as a negative example, perhaps—I learned from you the value of being there for them. But I can't thank you for that part.

What I can do, however, is forgive you. Your heart was good, but you had injuries, and you lacked good models yourself; these things all limited what you could do for me. I forgive you.

I was terribly sad to drop that dirt on your coffin. You were my father, and no matter what, I loved you. When that dirt fell, it meant there would be no chance to re-write our history, to heal it, to re-make it. No chance for you to be the father I needed and intuitively wanted. Our history died when you died.

Good-bye, Dad. May you rest in peace, and may I rest in peace.

Chris

HOW IS THAT POSSIBLE?

How is that possible?
How is it possible,
Across the field, he
Couldn't see me,
Couldn't hear me,
Turned suddenly and
Stared straight at me
Locking eyes.
How is that possible?

THE ROLE OF FAITH

It's easy to recognize the importance of faith for Christianity, Judaism, Islam, and Hinduism. Each of these religions have key beliefs and stories that their faithful accept. In contrast, although different Buddhist sects have their stories and traditions, faith generally is not as strongly associated with this religion. Zen Buddhists, in particular, fundamentally teach that each of us must discover the truth about our lives for ourselves; they rarely use the word "faith." Nevertheless, in this essay I consider the importance of faith even for Zen Buddhism.

For context and historical background, let's talk first about the opposite of faith. One word that frequently comes up is "doubt." In fact, this word is more commonly found than the word "faith" in traditional Zen literature. It is useful to explore how doubt is embedded in much of the Zen tradition (and in a non-spiritual way of life, for that matter)—and why faith is a natural and healthy alternative path.

In Zen, doubt (and confusion) is strongly associated with the study of koans, paradoxical riddles used as teaching tools. Koans are mostly culled from short accounts of an interaction between a teacher and student; they also include some commentary written by a teacher of long ago, which often doesn't make much more sense than the riddle itself. Those familiar with Zen Buddhist literature undoubtedly have encountered koans.

Koans basically take one of two forms. In their most common form, they are difficult to understand on an intellectual level, although their meaning can be intuited with the maturing of spiritual insight. They have some subtle logic, and in that sense, they can be viewed positively as a teaching instrument. The second type of koan is not meant to be understood at all on any level, either spiritual or intellectual. These koans exist only to frustrate the process of conceptual thought, in order to (hopefully) induce understanding and, eventually, enlightenment. Actually, enlightenment, or at least some deep understanding and growth, is the goal of both kinds of koans.

An example of a well-known Zen koan is something called the Great Matter. You may even see the term written in capital letters: THE GREAT MATTER. The Great Matter is understanding birth and death. It is often written out as: What is birth and death? Are you free of birth and death? Then there are the common corollaries: Are you afraid of death? Who were you before you were born? What happens when you die? And so on. That's the Great Matter.

A koan related to the Great Matter is: What are You? And there are other koans just as fundamental, such as... What is spiritual? What is meant by spirit? What is God, Buddha,

Allah? Does God exist? If I can't see or touch spirit, is it real? Are we just flesh and blood and guts, and that's all? When we die, is it simply "lights out"?

Are these questions easy to answer? Of course not! Whether or not you're a Zen student, imagine yourself being asked one of these questions. How would you answer, just as you are now?

Often, the reply is, "I don't know, but I'd really like to." Or simply, "Not sure. Don't know." Most of us don't know or aren't sure. Asking challenging questions like these stimulates and emphasizes doubt.

Perhaps after you have highly developed your spiritual practice, then you can answer questions like these. But in the meantime, another important consideration is whether asking these questions really helps us.

In some Zen traditions, students are encouraged to embrace and live day and night with "Great Doubt." This means living with doubt about our spirituality and about who or what we really are. Students are asked to think constantly about Great Doubt as a practice and a means to answering the Great Matter. With Great Doubt, there is no room for belief—it is necessarily excluded. The Zen adage "accept no dogma" is similar to "accept no belief"; dogma, after all, is the negative characterization of belief.

Clearly, some people are helped by holding Great Doubt in their minds; otherwise, the practice wouldn't have persisted over the centuries. However, I never received specific instruction about Great Doubt, and it sure didn't resonate personally. And as far as I could tell, studying koans did nothing for me. Moreover, while at the surface it may seem that there is no room for faith in Zen tradition, I actually have found faith to be a helpful lens through which to view Zen Buddhism—more helpful than koans or Great Doubt, in fact. Faith has been important to my path in Zen, which is not an easy practice with its long periods of silent and still meditation.

Faith is mostly missing from Zen literature, but there is one well-known exception which has been helpful for my practice. In his poem "Faith Mind," the ancient Chinese Zen teacher Sengstan instructs readers to have faith in the oneness of the world. (Interchange the words "trust" or "confidence" for "faith," as you prefer.)

> *To come directly into harmony with suchness,*
> *just simply say, when doubt arises, 'not two.'*
> *In this 'not two,' nothing is separate, nothing is*
> *excluded...*
> *to live in this faith is the road to non-duality,*
> *because the non-dual is one with the trusting mind.*
>
> *(Trans. Richard Clarke)*

Although Sengstan does not elaborate on "suchness," "the non-dual," or "not two," these Zen expressions teach that our nature is pure, we are one with the universe, and we are not separate from God or Buddha Nature. Non-duality also means that the ego has dissolved and there's no perception of being separate from others or our environment. Furthermore, with no self to defend, there is no fear. Consequently, there's no reason to search outside. The truth is not around the corner or in a distant monastery. It's not waiting for next year. It's right here today.

Sengstan's "not two" is perhaps a slightly different version of faith than, say, Christianity's. However, it also is an uplifting version of faith. When we feel out of sorts and out of harmony, we can center ourselves when we have faith in "not two." If you have confidence that you are not separate from God or the universe, a confidence that you can feel in your bones, even and especially if you haven't fully experienced that unity yourself—that's true faith.

There's one more reason to have faith that we are one with the divine. Doubt and confusion thrive in a dark, isolating place. In contrast, faith blooms in a bright and connecting place. Faith can relax us and allow us to feel safe and at peace, and that, in turn, can open our hearts to love. Perhaps that's why faith is so central to other religions. It should be central to Zen, as well. Instead of practicing Great Doubt, let us practice Great Faith.

CALIFORNIA AFTERNOON

Under the old oak tree,
Sun's power displayed
Reflecting on leaves while others shadowed.
A master's painting, no compromise.

Leaves drift slowly on the water
As a dragonfly
Rests on the iron rail.
Tiny particles of rust
Spark in the sunlight,
Burst into blossoms
As I descend
Into the cold creek.

Spiritual Reporter on the Celestial Washing Machine - Part 2

Star date June 2, 2019

It's about 10 days after my second psilocybin mushroom journey—10 days after another visit to the Celestial Washing Machine. When you enter the washing machine, it is important to remember you are the guest. You don't control what is going to happen, although you trust that the medicine is there to help you even if a difficult journey awaits. This reminds me of the well-known and highly experienced psychonaut Terence McKenna, who recalled saying to the earth medicine before ingesting: "I'm yours. Please don't hurt me." It doesn't matter how many times you've taken the journey; along with great respect, there always is going to be an element of trepidation. And this was just my second mushroom journey of my current era (psilocybin date 2 CE). There's no way I could even approach a feeling of confidence.

To make that very clear, as the effects were coming on after ingesting, I found myself chanting a mantra over and over: "I surrender. Please love me."

It's okay if you laugh at me for that. I probably patterned that mantra after McKenna's. But at the same time, know that I was serious and honest.

The setting was very similar to my previous journey's. The room was the same, the altar was about the same, and we held a similar ceremony with the cleansing smoking sage. I wrote new intentions onto a sheet of paper and placed it on the altar. After eating the mushrooms, I put on eyeshades and laid down on a mattress.

I wasn't looking specifically to heal my childhood trauma—that work felt pretty much completed—so my written intentions were very open-ended. They had two parts, plus a thank you at the end:

Surrender and go with the journey.
Whatever needs to be healed, let it please arise.

Please teach me. May I be a channel of your love and joy.

Thanks be to God!!

As my guide and I sat in front of the altar before our ceremony, he asked me if there was anything else I wanted to work on, perhaps something more specific. "Yes," I said. I told him I was feeling some self-doubt, not so much mentally, but in my body. Self-doubt, doubt of others, doubt of God, doubt about any and everything—this is a characteristic effect of childhood trauma. He said he thought some body and energy work would be helpful.

We raised the dried mushroom dose to 4.5 grams this time. Again, I slowly ate the mushrooms in the traditional Mexican way, adding a little occasional dab of honey, chewing finely with my front teeth and keeping the wet small bits in my mouth for a while before swallowing, often holding them under my tongue. Taking time in this way, I could feel the medicine begin to work while I was still eating.

As usual, my guide wrote down the things I said, keeping a partial record of my experience. Nearly every part of this journey had a common element, which gave this journey its title:

Journey into Pain

The journey began with music prompts played by my guide. Fairly early on, he played a female vocalist singing plaintively in a flamenco style. I said, "I can feel my wife's pain." She had had a difficult childhood, too, plus additional trauma as an adult, and I could really feel her pain. Feel it. Breathe it. And then I said I need to be careful and gentle with her.

At one point, my guide performed some deep body work on me. I verbalized what came out, shouting, and it was "PAIN!!"

Pain stored deep in my body was let loose. How much remains? I don't know, but after the journey I felt relief and peace, suggesting a great deal of pain was, in fact, released.

The next step was the one part of the journey that wasn't actually about pain. My guide wrote down my words: "It's okay to ask for love; I need it, too. A lot of people love me." What a beautiful thing for anyone to say. And the medicine is like truth serum. There is no BS with the plant medicine. So, given my traumatic childhood history and my life of doubt, expressing the belief that others love me shows how far I've come in my healing. Moreover, articulating that I need love and that it's okay to ask for it reveals authentic vulnerability—and vulnerability leads to liberation.

The music kept coming. There was a stretch of highly energetic music, excellent music to dance to, and, lying on my back with eyeshades on, that is what I did. I was moving my hands and arms in rhythm, really getting into the energy of the music. Great imagery and feeling washed over me, and I said, "I dance for people, for their pain; then, I can be part of their tribe. Taking in a lot of their pain. Taking the pain. It's so beautiful." Soon after, I said, "Coming to peace with feeling other people's suffering." And some time after that, I said, "To be a Bodhisattva, you have to be with other people's problems. Sometimes, there's nothing you can do for their pain; just be with them." The last sentence made me cry for the great suffering I could feel.

You don't normally associate peace and freedom with pain, with being vulnerable, with being open to others' pain. But being vulnerable is what makes us whole, connected, and that leads to peace. Not running away from, fearing, avoiding, or walling yourself off from other people's pain, or your own pain, as I so often did in the past.

I believe the divine is working with me, through me, helping me to help others, to take in their pain. It's providing the celestial energy to dance for their pain, connecting me to the tribe and the tribe to me and all of us together. I don't know if my words are working, but I hope this makes sense. I hope I am connecting to you.

There undoubtedly will be future journeys. There is plenty of room for me to continue to learn and grow. May I be the best Bodhisattva I can be. May all of you follow the Bodhisattva path, the path of serving all beings. And if Buddhism is foreign to you, perhaps instead think of sharing the love of Jesus, Mohammed, the Earth Mother, or the Universe as a way to take in your own and others' pain and radiate unconditional love.

SHARING WRITING

Sitting together, everyone sharing,
Sunlight covers the window.
We write, then pass,
Then pass and write,
Visions continue,
Visions changing,
Making poems like a path
With turns and straight lines,
Coming together, everyone sharing.
The statue and flowers
On the holy altar
Can't compare to my friends

LOVE AND BUDDHISM: CAN THEY GO STEADY?

Buddhism is known for two words in particular: wisdom and compassion. But the word LOVE is found infrequently, either in the literature or in dharma talks. Why is that?

To answer that question, let's examine some key Buddhist literature. Then, let's see what we can learn from other religious traditions—and even from pop culture! —that might help us reconcile Buddhist principles with love.

The Dhammapada, a collection of sayings in verse form, is one of the most widely read pieces in Buddhist literature. Part of the Pali Canon, the Dhammapada is more than 2,000 years old. It pre-dates both Mahayana and Zen Buddhism, and is attributed to the Buddha himself. It's relatively short, too, so there are many English translations (I checked some of them against each other for accuracy).

In chapter 16, titled "Affection," the Buddha speaks thusly about love:

210. Seek no intimacy with the beloved... for not to see the beloved is painful.

211. Therefore hold nothing dear, for separation from the dear is painful. There are no bonds for those who have nothing beloved.

212. From endearment springs grief, from endearment springs fear. From him who is wholly free from endearment there is no grief, when then fear?

213. From affection springs grief, from affection springs fear. From him who is wholly free from affection there is no grief, when then fear?

(Trans. Acharya Buddharakkhita)

Because this fundamental and early writing is attributed to the Buddha himself, it's easy to understand why subsequent Buddhist literature and tradition convey a similarly negative perspective on love and affection. In fact, this low view of affection, endearment, and intimacy has persisted in Zen Buddhism. We can see this in two examples from the revered literature. Dogen (born 1200 CE), the founder of the Japanese Soto sect of Zen Buddhism, wrote a collection essays known as the Shobogenzo. In his chapter "On Ceaseless Practice," Dogen said:

Even though we prize our relationships, such connections between ourselves and others are not things that can be held onto, so if we do not let go of our loved ones, chances are that our loved ones will let go of us, both in word and in deed...

Do not cling to love and affection, which is more foolish than the behavior of birds and beasts. Even if you are attached to feelings of love, they will not remain with you over the long years. (Gyōji)

(Trans. Rev. Hubert Nearman, O.B.C.)

Similarly, in his well-known poem "Faith Mind," the Third Zen patriarch Sengstan wrote:

The Great Way is not difficult
For those who have no preferences.
When love and hate are both absent
Everything becomes clear and undisguised.

(Trans. Richard Clarke)

Now one certainly can interpret these un-loving Buddhist quotations as expressing the wise principle of non-attachment. And from the practice of non-attachment, it's only a baby step—maybe not even a step at all—to the practice of mindfulness. Perhaps some Buddhists would scold me for misrepresenting the principle of non-attachment; and if I were to intimate in any way that there is some negativity ascribed to mindfulness, I would really be asking for it! Especially now that mindfulness has become mainstream—I would be called crazy. What's next? Criticizing yoga?

In fact, I'm not going to criticize mindfulness or non-attachment (or yoga). But in all seriousness, is it possible for anyone, especially a Buddhist, to practice non-attachment and love at the same time? Is it possible to practice mindfulness and love at the same time?

Please take a moment to ponder these questions, especially those of you who practice mindfulness and/or hold it in high esteem. How would you answer?

To bring the teachings of the Buddha, Dogen, and Sengstan into sharper focus, let's consider some non-Buddhist views on love and attachment.

Rumi, a Sufi mystic, was born in 1207 CE. He lived during the same medieval period as Dogen, and his poetry and prose about love remains popular today. Rumi wrote:

Your task is not to seek for love, but merely to seek and find all the barriers within yourself that you have built against it.

Wherever you are, and whatever you do, be in love.

Dogen went so far as to insult those who would embrace love, saying they were "more foolish than the […] birds and beasts." In contrast, Rumi embraced and exalted love, enjoining his readers to fill themselves and their world with love.

For Sengstan's counterpoint, let's look to the Bible. In the Gospel of Mark, Jesus/God says:

Love your neighbor as yourself.

Let us love one another, for love comes from God...
because God is love.

Again, we see a stark contrast between Sengstan's encouragement to abandon love and Jesus' claim that God is love. These words carry deep meaning. They lead us to different mindsets, different understandings of our place in the world and how to relate to this world and the people in it.

We can even mine contemporary pop culture for a different view on love. Juxtaposed against the Dhammapada's injunction to "hold nothing dear," we hear John Lennon singing, "All you need is love." In its simplicity, it is one of the most profound songs ever.

These are not silly or artificial comparisons. There is something serious to consider here, especially if you are a Buddhist, as I am. Although when I reflect on these passages, I find myself asking, "Am I really a Buddhist? Is this really Buddhism?"

Buddhists do have loving hearts, of course. However, while it is associated with compassion, traditionally, Buddhism has not been associated with love. What is the difference between compassion and love? Let's pause for a moment to talk about these two concepts. I like the definitions provided by Françoise Bourzat in her book Consciousness Medicine:

> *I consider love to be a state rather than an emotion. Its presence is naturally caring and concerned with the well-being, growth, and fulfillment of life. Love is a force that compels us to know ourselves more deeply and connect more fully with others. I am not talking about romantic love, nor am I speaking of sexual attraction. The kind of love I am talking about is similar to, but not the same as, compassion. Compassion tends to the vulnerability of humanity with an acknowledgment of the suffering of others, whereas love encompasses the greatness and celebration of all that we are. Love is our capacity to appreciate the complexity of others in all their dimensions. If a process is devoid of love, it is missing the core human element.*

Bourzat's definition of compassion, while brief, is in line with traditional Buddhist thought. We can elaborate slightly to say compassion is sympathy and concern for the suffering of others, with a motivation to relieve that suffering to the extent possible. I would enlarge Bourzat's definition of love. I believe love can be an emotion as well as a state of being. And while, like Bourzat, I do not include sexual attraction in my definition of love, I do include romantic love. My first thought was that only mature and securely attached couples illustrate my definition of love, especially since romantic love can "go wrong," resulting in mistreatment or divorce. But upon further reflection, I would not exclude any form of romantic love from my definition. I believe we all possess a basic human need to attach to a special person, and this impulse is born of love, and derives from divine love.

When we think deeply about these two concepts, we can find evidence that there is room in Buddhism—and yes, even in Zen Buddhism—for love as well as compassion. In the Theravada scriptures, there is a very popular teaching called the Metta Sutta, or, in English, the Loving Kindness Sutra. It is also recited in many Zen centers. Lines from one English translation of this sutra say:

> *With a boundless mind should one cherish all*
> *living things,*
> *Suffusing love over the entire world.*

That sounds wonderfully loving, doesn't it? The key word here is "metta." In Pali, the liturgical language of Theravada Buddhism, "metta" is most commonly translated as "loving kindness," and sometimes "goodwill" or "friendliness." Only occasionally is it translated as "love," as it is here. It seems some Buddhists are just plain afraid of the word "love," perhaps because of their long tradition of practicing non-attachment. Or is this avoidance also rooted in history?

Let's revisit those first lines from the Dhammapada ("Seek no intimacy with the beloved…"). I'm not convinced they were written or spoken by Buddha. More probably, they were written by a well-meaning priest (or committee of priests) in a monastery, long ago. He (not she!) was doing his best to articulate non-attachment; he was living a celibate life but failing to embrace his own humanness. And this patriarchal monastic mistake has carried on in Buddhism.

It's also important to consider the story, as we know it, of Gautama Buddha, and how he abandoned his wife and young child in order to seek enlightenment. The history says his wife and son later joined the (celibate) monastic order, but nevertheless, the family order was permanently broken. Perhaps it is here, in the story of the very origins of Buddhism, that we find the dismissive view of love that over the centuries has become foundational. Depending on your perspective, you could consider this a basic flaw in the religion, although perhaps 2500 years ago, in a much different setting from ours, it would have made sense.

Yes, it makes sense sometimes to retreat into dedicated practice, but should that retreat permeate Buddhist philosophy? Are Buddhists truly advised to abandon family and love?

I consider the avoidance—and, at times, outright rejection—of love to be mistaken. And it's time to correct this mistake. It's time to admit that parts of the old, cherished Buddhist literature can be well-meaning but wrong—or perhaps better said: unskillful for our time and place, not truly appreciative of what it means to be human. It's time to embrace a change in our understanding and no longer accept those passages. The world is nothing but change. Buddhism itself has endured much change, like the rise and passing of different teaching schools. Surely, we can adapt and embrace change where needed, bringing our essential humanness to reject select portions of the old literature.

So back to the question: Can you practice mindfulness and love at the same time? I will vote an emphatic yes! When you carefully observe your feelings, those feelings may be of love. Why not? You might even then experience joy in your heart. I hope you do.

We have an opportunity to enlarge our understanding of non-attachment and mindfulness. As our hearts grow big, let also our understanding grow big. We've been speaking of true love, authentic love, unconditional love. There are no bargains to be struck, no obligations to reciprocate feelings of love or any other emotions or actions. This principle of "no conditions" is the essence of non-attachment, no attachment.

You see, the Buddhist principle of non-attachment inherently fits within love. It's best practiced within love; it's best understood within love. We can even say that non-attachment is a pre-requisite to love. For love is selfless and giving, imbued with generosity and gratitude.

Now, finally, we can say, YES! Love and Buddhism can go steady. How? Because we can make it so. We're free to accept no dogma, free to ignore any literature or even history which no longer serves its purpose, which is no longer skillful for the setting. Free to decide that Love and Buddhism belong together. Free to love and practice mindfulness at the same time. Free to understand that the true meaning of non-attachment is to surrender to love and the wonders of life.

Mahatma Gandhi says, "Where there is love, there is life." Françoise Bourzat says, "Realize love as the force of creation." And I'll close by saying that the Bible got it right. The most profound, most important quotation for me is the one written above and repeated below: "Let us love one another, for love comes from God... Because God is love."

We can also say: Buddha is love, or Allah is love, or The Creator is love, or The Earth Mother is love, and so on, as you wish.

I'm all in. All in on God is love.

121

TWO THOUSAND YEARS

What is the message?
Unconditional love!
Love with no attachments
Love ascends the sky
Expands and fills all space
Love set free

Love thy neighbor –
You are my other self

Two thousand years of misunderstanding –
The story of Buddhist nonattachment,
Telling people not to love;
Two thousand years of Christian understanding –
Polluted by institutions that followed,
Love covered by attachments.

Patriarchal power structures,
Men in monasteries,
Message gets polluted,
Manners become twisted

Two thousand years, enough for evolution

Love comes from God
Because God is Love –
You are my other self

SPIRITUAL REPORTER ON THE (GROUP) CELESTIAL WASHING MACHINE - PART 3

Star date July 6, 2019

Journeys with earth medicine are by their very nature consciousness-expanding experiences. My previous journeys with sacred mushrooms were with only my guide present and took place inside a room in a house. What happens when the setting for the journey itself expands? What happens when there are others around you also journeying, who might make all sorts of noises or hear you make noises? What is it like when the only thing above your head is the night sky? What challenges or teachings will this expanded setting bring? I was to find out on this summer night.

Group journeys for healing and spiritual growth are an integral part of the traditions of the Huastec people of southern Mexico and other indigenous peoples in South America and Africa. In the newer and still developing Western practice of healing with psychedelics (entheogens), the group experience also has taken root. This adds the aspect of **community** that is missing in an individual journey. And when the experience takes place outside in a peaceful natural setting, it also adds the aspect of **environment** or **nature**.

Why does this kind of psychedelic medicine work in groups? We are social animals; we are psychologically designed to be within a community. Group energy is uplifting in inspirational or ritualistic occasions. This same effect occurs in meditation groups, drum circles, dance troupes—they produce a collective energy, encouraging participants to stay on the path. Journeying in a group also brings a natural connection to humanity. Every individual is at a different stage of development and has different needs, and yet every one is a truly valued member. Realizing this provides a warm, welcoming feeling, a feeling of safety. You aren't the only person in need of healing or spiritual growth. It's also humbling; you know that in the journey ahead, you might be the one calling out for help and displaying your vulnerability. These are all healthy, wonderful reasons to journey in a group—assuming the people in the group are well chosen and the group is under the care of a skilled and experienced guide-therapist. This certainly was the case for me.

We were a small group of five: three women and two men. Some groups are much larger. Four of the five of us were over 50 years old; three of us were over 60. Our leader was a man and his assistant guide was a woman, also well experienced. Our leader had a plan of activities in addition to the sacred psilocybin mushroom journey itself. He said he varies the plan somewhat from occasion to occasion. I can only describe our activities for this, my first group journey.

We arrived at a small clearing in a beautiful redwood forest, bringing the aspect of the environment to our group experience. The location was a short drive and a 15-minute hike in from our rendezvous spot. It was around noon on a lovely, warm summer day. The trees were extremely tall and stately. They were so big that we wondered whether they were "old growth" redwoods. I believe they were not—the ancient trees had been logged more than 100 years ago—but the tallest of these trees were still at least 200 feet (60 meters) tall. The outdoor setting was awe-inspiring!

We carried our sleeping bags, tarps, water, and food, along with our other supplies—eyeshades, toiletries, flashlights, writing materials, and items for a group altar. There were no tents. No toilets or outhouse, either. We shed our timepieces and turned off our phones. This was to be a truly outdoor journey.

We were instructed not to have any food or caffeine after 10 AM.

I noticed the two guides had taken off their socks and shoes and were walking barefoot on the forest floor after we arrived at our camp. I decided to join them, to feel closer to nature, to feel the earth beneath my feet.

We quickly set up our circle. The five of us journeyers arranged our sleeping bags around the altar, a small Mexican blanket placed on the ground. There was space on both sides of the altar for the two guides to sit. The altar had two Virgin Mary candles, some personal items, and a few Mexican shamanic objects, including a rattle, a feathered piece, part of the antlers from a small deer, a braid made of reeds, and a beaded necklace. A bunch of sage, tied with twine, rested in an abalone shell.

I brought a small Buddha carved from green stone, and a dense black rock from a beach in Santorini. The Buddha was holding a small pagoda, which houses sacred relics. The volcanic rock, smoothed by the crashing waves of the Aegean Sea, represented the earth and its great transformations. Other people brought crystals, shells, and a bust of the Buddha.

None of us had ever journeyed together, and we didn't know each other well at all. So, for our first community activity, each of us spoke for roughly ten minutes about why we were there and what our intentions were. Often, intentions are about what you want to heal or develop or understand: Where do I want to go? What do I hope to get out of the journey? People told brief stories about the pain in their lives and the symptoms that manifested for them. Several of us mentioned our "difficult" childhoods. Most of us were rather explicit during this revealing exercise, and it surely was the best thing we could have done to get to know each other and to understand with compassion the road each of us had walked. This truthfulness and vulnerability brought us together as a group.

I decided to begin with my intention, and then give my background. This was the reverse of how the others did it. Not sure why I decided to do it this way, but I did. My intention was "to grow as a Bodhisattva." Although I thought everyone in the group, including the non-Buddhists, would understand what that meant, the leader asked me to define the term. I explained that a Bodhisattva is someone dedicated to helping others—as a situation arises, as a situation calls for. I said that although my dreams reveal that I still need more healing, I believe I've done most of my healing from childhood trauma and that I have undergone a real transformation. And I told the group that since my second and most recent mushroom journey ("Celestial Washing Machine – Part 2"), I've felt that my energy now could be directed mostly toward helping others; I'm not so concerned with myself anymore.

After this short discussion of my intentions, I mentioned the trauma I experienced during my early childhood, and commented on how common it was—probably everyone in the group had suffered so. I described how I had used marijuana and alcohol to manage my pain, and that quitting alcohol was what brought me into psychotherapy. I also explained how my striving for success (resulting in a Ph.D. and an accomplished career) represented a typical attempt to win the love I didn't receive as a child. (Another person in our group told a similar tale of needing to over-achieve.)

It was not difficult to open up, to be revealing, and to be honest in the community setting. There was a real sense of safety and acceptance, honoring each other, and that helped us bond. But we weren't finished yet.

Our next activity was to build a nature altar. This exercise, meant to connect us with our environment, took about one hour and was done in silence. The leader picked a tree and we made the altar in front of it and on its bark, facing the path. We found pieces from the forest around us, and together we placed them on the altar, creating and decorating designs, working from each other's contributions. There were sticks and leaves of all sorts, pieces of moss, bark, redwood cones. We ended up with a beautiful woven tapestry of natural elements.

The next exercise was more community bonding and was performed to music. We paired up, stood still, and gazed into each other's eyes for a few minutes, while our guide spoke lyrics in a recitation style:

> *Here is a neighbor just like you who wants to*
> *be happy*
> *Just like you, just like me*
> *Here is a neighbor just like you who is a broken child*
> *Just like you, just like me*
> *Here is a neighbor just like you who longs for joy*
> *Just like you, just like me*
> *Here is a neighbor just like you who wants to be loved*
> *Just like you, just like me*

Then we switched partners, repeating the exercise until everyone had a turn with each other. This was a special bonding experience in a very personal way, and the lyrics helped us open our hearts to each other.

Now it was mid-afternoon. We were still hours before beginning the journey itself; the ingestion of the earth medicine was planned for shortly before sundown, and the summer day was long. We were still together following the heart-opening exercise, but our leader informed us that he wanted us to spend the rest of the afternoon alone. We were to separate, go a little way into the redwoods, and mindfully create a Deathbed from the forest material. Then we would lie down in that bed and prepare for death. Our leader would ring a bell when it was time to return to our camp, in about three hours.

There were several trails in the area, and I followed one for a ten-minute barefoot walk. When you are looking for a place to die, you select it mindfully, carefully. Not just any place will do for such an important event. I looked around as I walked down the narrow path, until I came across a picturesque clearing. The left side of the path was very pretty, but there was a slope to the ground and I decided I wanted a flat bed. On the other side of the path, there was a small open area, thick with redwood needles and flanked by lush ferns. I felt this would be a good place to die.

I took my time feeling the environment around me. I decided a very simple bed "frame" was all I needed. I constructed a simple rectangular border from the available forest material. On the two long sides, I used twigs and small branches shed from the redwoods. For the head and foot of the border, I used some bark, and I decorated it with very small redwood cones, about a half-inch across. I cleared the area within the border of obvious debris, leaving primarily just the redwood needles.

Then, I sat down on the soft bed of redwood needles. I rested there for a while, getting a feel for the bed and the surroundings. I spent considerable time looking at the trees— their beauty, and how the dappled sunlight brought out the colors of the redwood bark and the green branches. I heard some birds singing.

When I was ready, I lay down. I took in the forest around me from this new perspective, looking directly up at the tall redwoods. After more time passed, I was ready to begin my good-byes.

I began with my two children. I spoke to them in my mind, telling them how much I loved them and that I hoped they would live long lives with much happiness. I said I was sorry for the mistakes that I had made, but that overall, I was content with all the love I gave them. I accepted that my life would slowly fade from their memories.

Next, I said goodbye to my wife. I told her how glad I was that we walked back from the precipice of distrust, that we both realized the trauma of our childhood and took brave action. I recalled how we took insights from talk therapy and leapt into the unknown by taking journeys with the help of powerful medicine, traveling to the source of our disconnections. We let love heal our deep wounds. I told her how grateful I was that we waited patiently for each other to be whole again.

Then, I said farewell to my brothers. They kept me sane in childhood, although being the youngest, I was sometimes the object of their frustration and pain. I thanked them for our secure bond and wished them some of the healing that I have experienced. I wished them peace and happiness.

My friends came last, and there were quite a few. I called out to each of my close friends one by one, hoping I wasn't forgetting any. I told each of them how important they were to me and how I loved them. I thanked them for our sharing and learning together, for just being together, accepting each other, making life more complete.

Then I lay quietly, looking up into the trees. I noticed the sun was getting lower and most of the light was blocked by the forest. I started to feel a chill. The temperature was dropping quickly, now; it was getting closer to sunset. I felt both satisfaction with and some sadness about my goodbyes. I felt I was ready to let go and let the earth take me back.

A distant bell called. Closer, it rang. I sat up and turned to look behind me. Our leader was walking toward me, coming to bring me back to the group, to the unknown journey into life and death that awaited that night, to a place I couldn't anticipate, couldn't predict. A journey of healing and insight, I hoped. I sensed it would be a difficult journey.

The group gathered and the leader explained how we would proceed. We each would come up to the side of the altar where he was sitting and receive our medicine. The assistant guide sat on the other side of the altar, watching closely. Our leader would ring a bell about an hour after we ate, signifying the start of the group journey, and he would ring the bell again at the end of the journey, roughly six hours after that, or whenever he felt the time was right.

We came up one by one and kneeled before our guide to receive our medicine. He had a small portable electronic scale in front of him, and a bag of beautiful, intact dried psilocybin mushrooms. He asked each of us what weight of mushrooms we wanted. He and I had talked about this beforehand; I imagined each of us had done so. But of course, as the moment came, we could change our minds. The magnitude of the dose is of consequence, of course. We had discussed 5 grams for me, and I stayed with that number.

We each sat with our legs inside our sleeping bags. It was now quite chilly, and the day's heat was leaving through the clear, blue sky above us. Sunset was close and the light dimming. We held our mushrooms on our laps, slowly ingesting our medicine in the traditional Mexican manner, chewing only with our front teeth, holding the mushrooms in our mouth until well wet before swallowing. Our other guide came around periodically with a jar of semi-solid honey that we could dip our finger into and add a little sweetness as we ate.

It takes some time to eat 5 dried grams in this way, but it was not difficult or unpleasant for me. This was a sacred partaking of the earth's medicine. A blessing and an honor to be given the opportunity, to be accepted as part of the group. It was a ceremony that affirmed our awe of the mystery of life.

As evening descended, the only light came from two Virgin Mary candles. After eating, we laid down in our sleeping bags and put on our eyeshades. Although we were in our circle and could hear each other, this was going to be a solo trip for each of us.

It doesn't take long to begin to feel the effects when you eat the mushrooms in this way. The journey was clearly beginning, punctuated by a few yawns, a common symptom of going up as well as coming down. I knew I was already setting out on the journey when I heard the bell marking the official start for the group.

Here is my trip report. It's briefer than what you might expect from a six-hour journey, but these are the highlights that I recall.

At the outset, I really did feel like I was being tossed around by the agitator of the Celestial Washing Machine. I don't know what my body was doing, but I was feeling as though I was being twisted and contorted this way and that. I know I was being cleaned by the medicine. It wasn't comfortable, but I was okay with it. Our leader came by, knelt by my side and whispered in my ear, "How are you doing? I told him, "I'm well. I'm cleaning" (meaning, I was being cleaned). He patted me, and, seeing that I was fine, went to check on the next person.

When you're on the journey, the concept of time generally disappears—but I know I was in the Celestial Washing Machine's agitator for quite a long period. What exactly was being cleaned, I couldn't say, but I know that was what was happening. The medicine was cleaning me and healing me.

Then, there was a shift. I became calmer. I felt I was drifting upward to the stars, to the heavens. I came back to my intention, but instead of "May I grow as a Bodhisattva," I began saying to myself, "Please make me a channel of your love, make me a channel of your love." Then, I was in the presence of the supreme being. It wasn't a man with a white beard; it was some sort of mystical understanding, ineffable. I said, "Make me a channel of your love." An answer came back: "Then you have to die." And with that, I dissolved into the heavens. I was no more.

There were stars. There was beauty. There was the divine. There was love.

I believe most of the journey was up in the stars, which were literally above us in the clear night. Eventually, I felt that I was coming back into a body, reassembling a bit at a time. I remember not really caring if I was going to be in a body again.

I remember my neighbor making some noise, having a challenging journey. (It turned out well for her, I can report.) The thought arose: *I wonder if she's dying*. Then the thought arose: *Maybe I'm dying too*. If so, it didn't seem to matter. I didn't care at all. There was no fear.

Around this time, the leader came over and did some body work on me, which felt great. I was totally pliant. He also did energy work, probing and feeling the energy flowing through my body.

Soon after, I was coming down. I felt peaceful. Our guide played some perfect music for us. Here are some partial lyrics of three of the songs that I remember:

The whole world is a very narrow bridge
And the most important thing
Is to have no fear at all

—*Rabbi Nachman of Breslov*

La ilaha illa Allah
Everything is God and God is everything

—*Muslim prayer, loosely translated*

You have to humble yourself in front of the medicine
You gotta bend down low
You have to humble yourself in front of the medicine
Ask it what it knows.

We shall lift each other up
higher and higher
We shall lift each other up.

—*Rainbow hippie song*

Then the bell rang, signifying the end of the journey. The most intense part was over. Six or so hours had passed since the first bell. Before we began the journey, our leader had asked if anyone wanted to sing when we were done. I had raised my hand, thinking it would be some sort of sing-along. Instead, he said to me, "Sit up and sing." I had no idea what to sing. No song was in my head. I heard my fellow journeyers, and I said, "I hear your beautiful voices." And there was some laughing, some happy, warm feelings. Then someone said, "I love you, Chris." I said, "Thank you." Then I sang "Beautiful Love." I believe I actually created the melody, singing, "Beautiful, beautiful love." Those were the only two words. The song probably lasted a minute.

Next, our two guides placed snack food in the middle of our circle, the two candles providing all our light. All vegetarian food, of course. Mostly fruits and nuts. We needed some nourishment after the long and strenuous journey we all had experienced, and we hadn't eaten since before 10 AM. It was now probably 2 AM or so, the following day. There was some talking as we gathered closer, eating, sharing. Clearly, there was a wonderful, loving feeling between all of us journeyers.

Next was sleep. We settled back in our bags to get some well-earned rest.

In the morning, we gathered in a tight circle. The guides brought out more food, and we shared and ate well. The food tasted delicious.

After we all helped clean up, we sat in a circle a little way away from our camp. It was time to share our journey experiences. One by one, the five of us reported, taking about ten minutes each. After each person spoke, each of the other journeyers would respond with something supportive and loving, often with detail and insight, although sometimes with just a simple "I love your smile," or "You were so brave." Then, the guides would say something. I knew I should go last as I could sense that I was the only one on this particular journey to have had a full-blown mystical experience. It just seemed appropriate to go last.

After reporting my experience, the leader said that I was what some spiritual cultures call a warrior, someone who fearlessly seeks the divine. He also said that when he checked my body energy, the energy was freely flowing through me. Like a channel, I suppose. I took those comments as validation that I am making progress in becoming a serving Bodhisattva. But it's a path, and I know I have more distance to tread.

After our sharing, we packed up our camp, and hiked back to our cars where we hugged and said our good-byes.

Integration work with the leader subsequently followed, as is customary and needed after every journey. Writing is also part of the integration process for me.

All in all, I am so thankful for our guides, my fellow journeyers, the earth medicine, the wonderful mystical experience, and the love I bathed in and feel now.

This journey into the Celestial Washing Machine was all the more rewarding because of the community we formed beginning before and continuing after. And the environment of the grand redwood forest—with earth below us, sky above us— formed a nurturing container where life and death could both dissolve and healing and spiritual growth could emerge.

TWO DEATH POEMS

SWIFT CLOUDS AND THE JEWEL HARE

At ninety-nine, snowy side-locks,
Beard, a thin-shouldered, fur-robed one
Has cut all earthly ties. Laughing, I point
To the swift clouds. Jewel Hare blazes over all.

—Gen of Kohoin (d. 1085)
From: Zen Poems of China and Japan: The Crane's Bill
(Trans. Lucien Stryk and Takashi Ikemoto)

DEATH MASK

At ninety-one, Mother Audrey
Thin as from Dachau
Clinging, calling "Mother! Help me! Help me!"
Suddenly rising in bed as if from death
Yet more dying to do, ever so slowly
With spasm and gasp
Until finally mouth agape
Breath escaped her ashen face.

BED IN THE WOODS

In the redwood forest
I made a bed to lie in.
The mattress was soft,
A thick mat of redwood needles.
I lay a border for the bed;
On the two long sides
I put twigs and small dead branches;
For the head and foot I placed
A little bark and redwood cones.
A few feet to one side was a narrow path,
On the other side green ferns.
I laid down on the bed to die.
I didn't know how long it would take.
I looked up at the tall redwood trees,
Stately and strong,
With little redwood trees surrounding.
Dappled summer sunlight kissed the
Redwood bark and green branches
Making their colors glow.
Sunlight kissed my face too, but briefly.
I wasn't sure if it was saying hello or goodbye.

Then it was time to get on with it,
Time to say my goodbyes.
I started with my two kids.
I told them how much I loved them,
How I tried hard to be a good dad,
Did mostly a good job,
Was sorry for the mistakes.

I wished them a happy long life,
Thought they'd miss me but
Would have wonderful lives
While I'd slowly fade into memories.
My wife was next
And the sentiments and love similar,
Especially glad we found a way to
Grow together, heal together.
My brothers, one by one, followed.
I told them I loved them and
Wished them happier days.
Close friends came last but not least.
I told them how much I loved them, too
And thanked them for their long friendships,
Glad we could share and learn from each other.

Soon the sun descended in the sky
And the temperature cooled.
As evening approached
I settled into my deathbed.
It wasn't until later that night
Under the shining stars
Between the tall trees
That death finally arrived.